Practical Fishing Tips

MINNETONKA, MINNESOTA

During his extensive travels as an outdoor writer and multispecies fisherman, author Dick Sternberg has discovered a goldmine of little-known fishing tips and tricks that are sure to make you a more successful angler.

Practical Fishing Tips

Mike Vail
Vice President,
Product & Business Development

Tom Carpenter
Director of Book Development

Dan Kennedy
Book Production Manager

David Schelitzche
Book Design & Production

Gina Germ
Photo Editor

Michele Teigen
Senior Book Development Coordinator

Bruce Holt
Janice Cauley
Proofreading

Tip Contributors

Dan Gapen	Dick Sternberg
Paul Hartman	Mike Hehner
Jim Moynagh	Mike McClelland
Chris Winchester	Dick Grzywinski
Bill Lindner	

Principle Photography
Bill Lindner Photography (Bill Lindner, Mike Hehner, Tom Heck, Pete Cozad, Jason Lund)

Additional Photography
Dick Sternberg pp. 19, 34, 39, 44, 74(2), 75(2), 76, 122, 125, 127
Sportsman's Guide pp. 62, 65
Jon Storm p. 106
©MN DNR p. 107
Dan Kennedy pp. 24, 113
Daniel Stair/Luhr-Jensen p. 127
Greg Fisher/Outdoor Innovations p. 135

Illustration
Bill Reynolds pp. 18, 20 all, 23 both, 33, 36 all, 44, 45 all, 46, 56, 65, 66, 67, 76 both, 77 all, 79, 85 both, 95, 105, 107, 108, 116 both, 122, 123, 125, 135 both, 137
Dave Schelitzche pp. 27 both, 60, 81, 103, 126, 153

9 8 7 6 5 4 3 2 1
ISBN 1-58159-080-6

North American Fishing Club
12301 Whitewater Drive
Minnetonka, MN 55343

CONTENTS

INTRODUCTION

Okay, I'll admit it. I've had a backlash before. I've also had knots fail (on some *very* nice fish), experienced problems with line twist, and had to relaunch my boat to get it evenly on the trailer. We've all done things like this—sometimes more than once!

So your Club created *Practical Fishing Tips*. Though this book may not win awards for creative writing, you will deem it an award winner when you start putting all these tips, tricks and techniques to work.

Keep *Practical Fishing Tips* handy and refer to it often. Now you have a place to turn to when fishing's little (and big) problems arise.

Do you know how to replace a broken line guide? Eliminate twisted line? Activate lethargic leeches? Store trotlines? Spool line correctly on a spinning reel? Separate stuck rod sections?

Practical Fishing Tips answers all this and much, much more.

Author Dick Sternberg has spent a lifetime fishing, and has been compiling tips from top anglers for more than 40 years. Every idea here has been time tested and Sternberg-approved on the water; these ideas will help you avoid common problems, and in many ways just do things better.

My only wish is that this book had been available at every stage of my fishing career. Even now, in these pages, I'm still finding fishing wisdom I'll be putting to good use.

Enjoy!

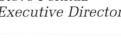

Steve Pennaz
Executive Director

EQUIPMENT TIPS

*F*ine-tuning your equipment can make a huge difference in your fishing success.

ROD & REEL TIPS

If you do a lot of fishing, there's no way to avoid rod and reel problems. You'll have to deal with sticky drags, grooved line rollers, broken guides, loose tips and rod sections that get stuck together. You could probably find someone to cure these headaches for you, but most of them are easily fixable—if you know how.

Here are some tips for solving the most common rod and reel problems, along with a few suggestions for improving your tackle's performance.

NO-STICK DRAG

Many inexpensive spinning reels have sticky drags, especially if the drag adjustment is at the rear rather than the face of the reel. And that sticky drag can cost you the fish of a lifetime.

You could try replacing the drag washers to smooth out the drag, but it will probably start to stick again. Here's a sure cure:

Tighten your drag down completely so it won't slip at all, and make sure your anti-reverse is off. Then, when a good-sized fish makes a run, just reel backward. If you can't keep up with the fish, let go of the handle and feather the spool with your fingers to prevent an overrun. Most pro fishermen use the backreeling method rather than relying on the drag, even with expensive reels. If you're fishing for fast-running fish like salmon however, you'll have to rely on your drag because you can't backreel fast enough.

NO MORE FRAYED MONO

If the mono on your spinning reel seems to be fraying more than normal (inset), the culprit is probably a grooved line roller on the bail.

Grooves are most common on older reels with stainless-steel rollers and are caused by line wear. They can fray your line to the point where it breaks with only a slight tug.

A groove may not be easy to see with the naked eye. Use a magnifying glass to check the roller, and replace it if necessary. Any sporting goods store with a reel repair service can supply the roller, but it may be an item they have to order.

SNAG-RESISTANT ROD

When fishing on a rocky bottom, most anglers try to minimize hang-ups by using snag-resistant sinkers and hooks. But no sinker or hook is 100% snag-free.

Here's how to further cut down on hang-ups when fishing rocky cover:

Use an extra-long rod (8-foot-plus) that enables you to change your angle of pull much more than you could with a short rod. This way, you can work your way around the snag to find the angle that allows you to pull free—without moving your boat.

SEPARATING ROD SECTIONS

Two-piece rods are not as popular as they once were, but many anglers still like them because they fit into a short rod box and are great for travelling.

But if you've ever owned a two-piece, you know the rub: The sections get stuck together and no matter how hard you pull, you can't separate them.

The longer you keep the sections together, the harder it is to pull them apart.

Here are two ways to solve this "sticky" problem:

Method 1. *Lay some ice cubes on the ferrule and wait 10 minutes or so. The ice shrinks the ferrules and they can usually be separated easily.*

Method 2. *While holding the rod behind your knees and grasping it firmly, spread your knees to separate the sections.*

STORING TWO-PIECE RODS

When storing a two-piece rod, you'll want to bundle the fragile tip section with the stiff butt section to prevent breakage. You could tape the sections together but that leaves the sections caked with messy adhesive. Here's a better way:

Hook a heavy rubber band around a guide, wrap it around both sections several times and then hook it over the guide again. A pair of rubber bands secured this way will keep the sections together.

ICE-RESISTANT ROD TIP

If you do a lot of ice fishing or other cold-weather angling, you've no doubt been bothered by your rod tip constantly freezing up. The ice is difficult to remove because it collects on the struts (right) where you can't flick it off with your fingers. You could solve the problem by sticking the tip in your mouth to melt the ice, but here are a couple of better ideas:

Fly Rod Tip. Heat your rod tip to melt the ferrule cement, remove it and then replace it with a fly rod tip of the same diameter. You may have to add some more ferrule cement to secure it. A fly rod tip has no struts to collect ice; when it freezes up, you can easily de-ice it with a flick of your fingers.

Chapstick Coating. Smear some Chapstick or Vaseline on all your rod guides, making sure you coat the inside surface. The slippery guides resist ice formation and even if a little ice does build up, you can easily flick it away.

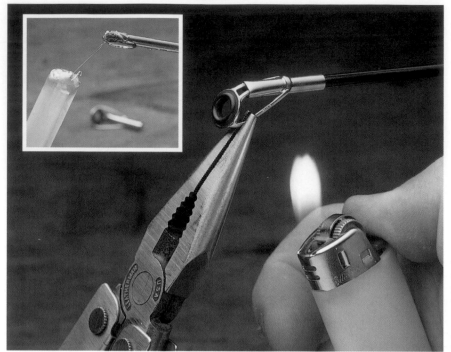

SOLID CEMENT

You can easily replace a broken rod tip using ferrule cement, but you may have trouble getting the cement to hold because you push it off when seating the tip. Here's the solution:

Apply cement to the end of the rod (inset), push the tip on partway, then hold it with needlenose pliers while heating it with a lighter. When the heat draws the cement into the tip, push it on the rest of the way.

QUICK FIX FOR LINE WRAPS

It's amazing how a wrap of line can mysteriously appear around your rod when you're fishing (right). The wrap fouls up your casting and makes it nearly impossible to reel in a fish.

You could remove your lure and restring the rod, but there's a much easier fix:

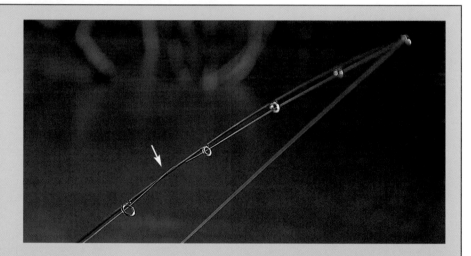

1 *Pull on the wrapped line to form a large loop and then pass the loop around the lure and the end of the rod tip as shown.*

2 *Now the line wrap is gone and you can resume fishing.*

EMERGENCY ROD HOLDER

If you troll, you probably use rod holders so you can fish with multiple lines. If you're a still fisherman, rod holders prevent your rod from being pulled into the lake.

But what if you forget your rod holders at home or are using a rental boat? Here's a way to improvise (assuming you can find some PVC pipe and duct tape):

Find a piece of PVC pipe with a diameter large enough for your rod handle and then tape it to one of the struts on the side of the boat. The strut holds the rod at the perfect angle.

ROLLER GUIDE FOR WIRE LINE

Stainless-steel wire line is popular among deep-water trollers because it gets down in a hurry and has no stretch. But it will eventually wear a nasty groove in your rod tip (right) that can damage the wire or cause it to bind. Here's the best answer:

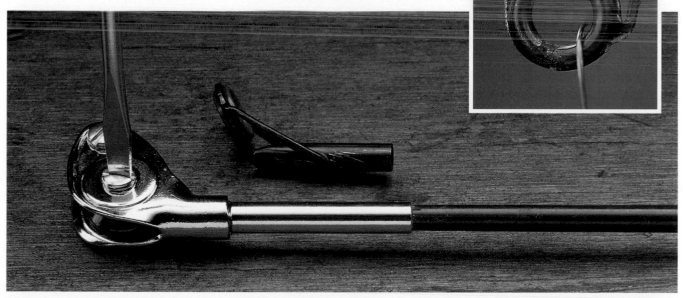

Remove your rod tip and replace it with a roller-tip of the same diameter. Some roller-tips have tension screws; if the roller is not spinning freely, adjust the screw.

HOW TO REPLACE ROD GUIDES

Anybody who does a lot of fishing will eventually have to replace a broken, grooved or loose rod guide. You could have a custom rod shop do the job, but that is likely to be expensive and they may not be able to get to it for months. Here's how to fix the rod yourself:

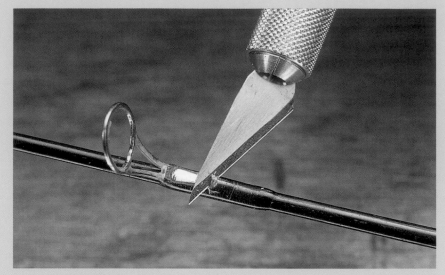

1 Remove the old guide by cutting the windings with a razor blade. Take care not to nick the rod itself.

2 Place the rod in a winding jig (left) which has a rod holder and a spindle that keeps tension on the spool of winding thread. If you don't have a jig, cut v-shaped grooves in a cardboard box and run your thread through the pages of a phone book to maintain adequate tension (right).

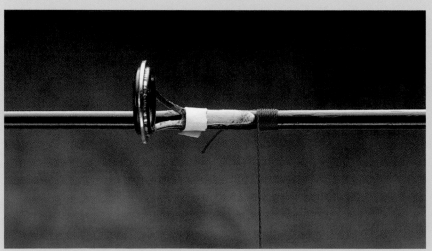

3 If you're using a double-foot guide, tape down one foot to hold the guide in place while you start to wrap the other. With a single-foot guide (shown), use a thin strip of tape near the eye. Begin your wraps about 1/4 inch from the end of the foot, turning the rod to wrap the thread. The wraps should be tight and even, with no overlaps. When the wraps have secured the guide, remove the tape.

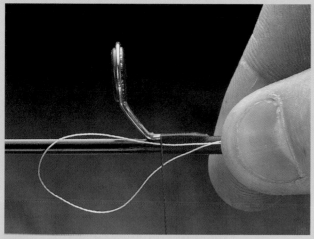

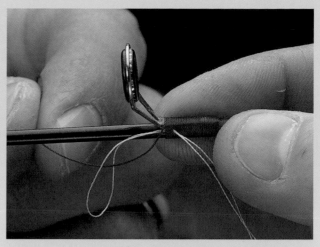

4 *When you have wrapped to within about ¹/₁₆ inch of the end, lay down a separate loop of thread as shown and then finish wrapping. Be sure to leave a tag end several inches long.*

5 *While holding the wraps with your fingers, put the tag end through the loop.*

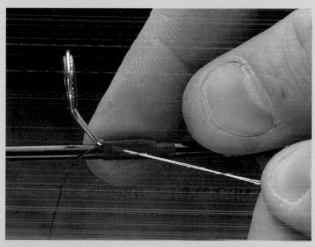

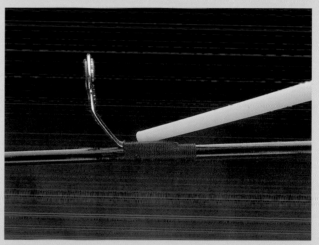

6 *Pull the loop of thread to draw the tag end beneath the wraps and out the side of the windings. Closely trim the tag end.*

7 *Even out the windings and remove any gaps using the handle of a paint brush.*

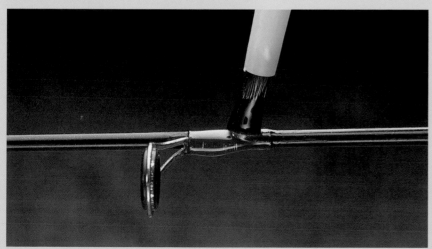

8 *Turn the rod with one hand while using your brush to apply epoxy rod-winding finish with the other. To prevent drips from forming, turn the rod frequently during the first hour after application. Let the finish dry overnight and then apply another coat. If necessary, trim off any hardened drips with a razor blade before applying the second coat of finish.*

BREAK THE BACKLASH HABIT

Whether you call them backlashes, bird's nests or "professional overruns," these untimely tangles cause fits for practically all anglers who use baitcasting gear.

Although there is no way to eliminate this headache altogether, you can keep backlashing to a minimum with the tips shown on these pages.

Use Correct Spool Tension. Adjust your spool tension to match the weight of the lure you're casting. While holding the rod horizontally, turn the tension screw until the lure drops slowly from its own weight.

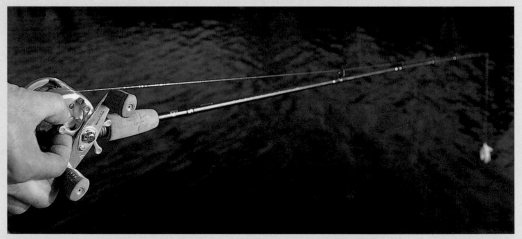

Narrower Is Better. The narrower the spool, the less likely it is to backlash. A narrow spool (left) is lighter than a wide one (right), so it has less momentum and is not as likely to keep spinning at the end of the cast.

Tape Block. *Make the longest cast you can, lay a strip of electrical tape across the spool and then wind the line back in. Now, even if you do get a backlash, it won't go below the level of the tape.*

Use Thumb Tension. *Thumb the spool if necessary to prevent an overrun as the spool is spinning in mid-cast, and increase the thumb tension to stop the spool just as the lure lands.*

Don't Cast Into Wind. *Avoid casting directly into the wind. The wind resistance slows the flight of your lure (shown) so it does not take out line as fast as the spool is spinning. The final result: a backlash. If you must cast into the wind, keep your casting trajectory low.*

BOAT & MOTOR TIPS

Even though fishing boats and motors are constantly improving, innovative anglers always seem to come up with ways of making their boats more functional or improving their performance. Here are some tips for selecting the boat and motor that best suits your style of fishing, rigging it to suit your specific needs and solving some of the most common boat-owners' headaches:

FLOW-THRU LIVE WELL

Many jon boats come with a live well built into the center seat. The live well fills through a hole in the bottom from the weight of gear and passengers. But the single hole allows for little water circulation and, when the boat tips to one side, much of the water runs out.

To ensure good circulation and an adequate water level, select a boat with two holes in the live well. This way, the water can enter one hole and spill out the other as the boat rocks from side-to-side. And the level always stays high.

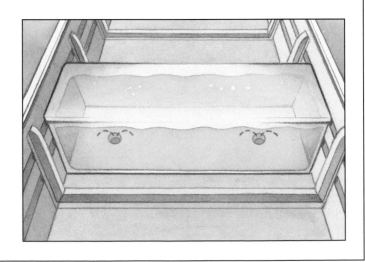

REMOVING STICKY SEATS

Many modern fishing boats come with interchangeable seats—the ones with the plastic bases and the snap-in tabs. It's easy to understand why these seats are so popular because you can customize your seat configuration to suit the number of passengers and the type of fishing you will be doing.

There's just one problem: These seats tend to stick and even a weight lifter can't pull hard enough to free the seat from its base.

Don't make the mistake of spraying the plastic with WD-40 or any other lubricant. If you do, the seat will slip out of the base, and the passenger will wind up on the floor.

Here's the best way to loosen sticky seats:

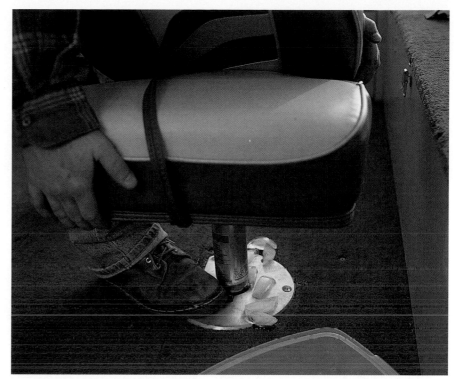

Place a layer of ice cubes around the top of the plastic insert and wait about 10 minutes for the insert to contract before attempting to remove the seat. Then use your toe to hold in the tab and pull straight up on the seat while rocking it back and forth. It should pop right out.

PRESERVE YOUR CARPET

It's nice to have a carpeted boat, but the carpeting soon gets filthy from sand, mud, squashed bait and fish slime.

And if you use your boat a lot, the carpeting around the driver's seat will probably wear thin.

Here's how to keep your carpet looking (and smelling) good:

Cover the original carpeting on the floor of your boat with rubber-backed carpeting intended for outdoor use. If you have an elevated casting deck, cut two pieces: one for the deck and one for the floor. Make a cutout for each seat base. When the carpet gets dirty, take it out and spray it down with a hose. Replace the carpeting after it dries.

BIG-WATER HULL

Many big-water anglers buy deep-hulled boats, assuming that the extra depth will keep them dry in heavy seas. But they're often disappointed (and soaking wet) when the deep hull fails to keep out the spray.

Experienced large-lake fishermen know that the shape of the hull is even more important than the depth. The key is a flared hull, as the cross-section diagrams (left) illustrate.

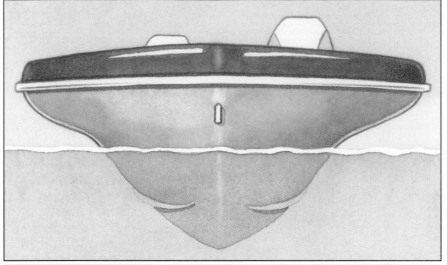

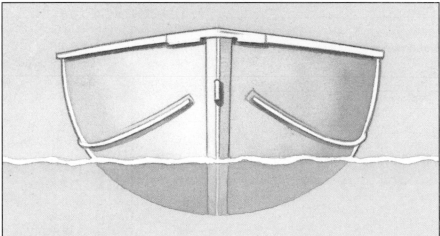

A flared hull (top) deflects spray to the side so it doesn't blow back into the boat as it does with a smooth, rounded hull (bottom). Many big-water anglers prefer fiberglass hulls because they can be molded into the ideal flared shape.

TUNNEL JON FOR SHALLOW WATER

A jon boat, because of its flat bottom, is a great choice for very shallow water. But many anglers do not realize that they can navigate even shallower water with a "tunnel jon." Because of the cutout in the bottom (left) the propeller does not ride below the bottom of the boat, making it possible to run in water only a few inches deep without damaging the prop.

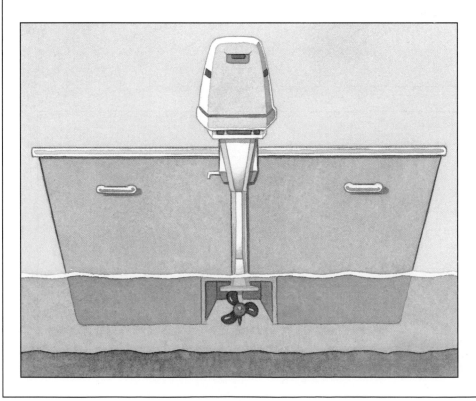

MAXIMIZE OUTBOARD POWER

Most anglers know that a shallow boat takes a short-shaft outboard while a deep boat requires a long-shaft. But if you want to maximize the performance of your outboard, you'll have to be a little more precise.

If the shaft is too long, it extends too far beneath the bottom of the boat, causing drag that reduces your speed and increases fuel consumption. If it's too short, the hull restricts the flow of water to the prop, so the motor over-revs and loses power. If you own a small boat and motor, you can detect and fix the problem quite easily:

1 With your boat on the trailer, check the height of your cavitation plate. It should line up with the bottom of the boat (dotted line).

2 If the cavitation plate is too low, set a board on top of the transom and reattach the motor. If the motor is bolted to the transom, reattach it to lower holes in the bracket. If the plate is too high, your best option is to install a "jackplate" to the transom so the motor rides lower.

LEVEL LOADING

Those drive-on trailers make loading your boat a breeze, but if your trailer isn't level on the ramp, you may find that your boat is sitting cockeyed when you pull it out of the water (above). Here's how to compensate for an uneven launching ramp:

If your trailer is tilted to the left, drive your boat to the right when loading. If it's tilted to the right, drive your boat to the left. This way, the boat will rest nearly level on the trailer.

CROSS YOUR CHAINS

Should your boat trailer somehow slip off your hitch, safety chains will keep the trailer attached to your vehicle, preventing a serious accident (inset). The problem is, your trailer tongue might drop to the ground, possibly causing serious damage to your trailer.

Here's an easy way to prevent that from happening:

Cross your safety chains or cables (left); this way, they form a "cradle" that will catch your trailer tongue should the trailer become disconnected from the hitch.

FINE-TUNE TONGUE WEIGHT

How well your rig rides on the highway depends, to a large extent, on "tongue weight," meaning how much downward force the tongue of your trailer exerts on the hitch.

Too little tongue weight could cause the trailer to veer from side-to-side; too much puts excessive weight on the hitch, making your vehicle ride too low in the rear.

Here's how to fine-tune your tongue weight for a perfect ride:

Estimate the total weight of your boat, motor and trailer. Calculate 5 to 10 percent of that amount (weight x .05 or .10) and then set the trailer tongue on a bathroom scale to see if the tongue weight is in the right range. If not, you'll have to loosen up the bolts on your winch stand, slide it backward or forward to change the trailer's balance and adjust other supports accordingly.

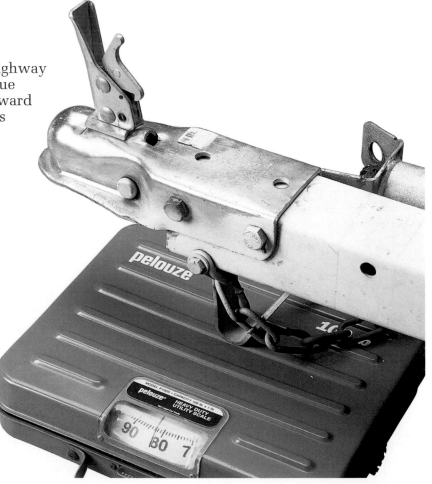

TROLL AT ANCHOR

When you're fishing at anchor, it's difficult to put your boat exactly where you want it. Sometimes you miscalculate when trying to judge where the wind will take the boat, so you wind up a little to one side or the other of the desired spot.

Rather than repositioning the boat several times to get on the spot, give this a try:

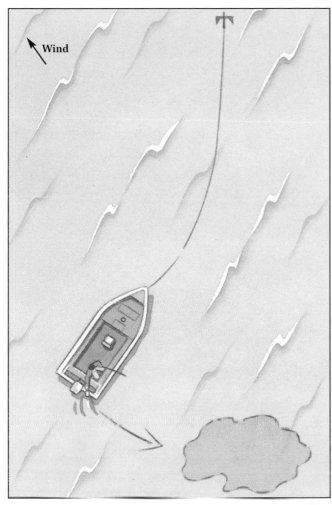

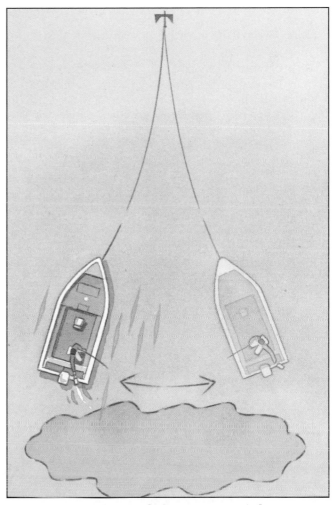

Stop your boat directly upwind or upcurrent of the area you want to fish (shaded zones above), let out considerably more anchor rope than you ordinarily would and attach the rope to the bow eye. After the boat settles into position, use a transom-mount trolling motor to adjust the position laterally. This way, you can compensate for shifting winds (left) or pull the boat from one side to the other to cover a larger area (right).

TRIM UP FOR SLOW TROLLING

"Bigger is better" seems to be the current trend in outboard motor selection. But many anglers are finding that they can't troll as slowly as they'd like with these big outboards.

Before you buy a "kicker" motor to solve the problem, try this:

Trim up your outboard as high as you can without lifting the prop out of the water. With the motor tilted this way, it has considerably less power so it trolls more slowly.

BOAT-STORAGE TIPS

If you live in a cold climate and have to store your boat over the winter, serious problems can develop with your boat, motor and trailer if your rig is not properly winterized.

Here are some simple steps to ensure that your boat runs smoothly come spring:

1 Replace the oil in your lower unit. If water has seeped in, it will freeze and crack the housing. Remove the bottom filler screw in the lower unit, insert the tip of a lubricant tube, remove the top filler screw (inset, arrow) and then squeeze the tube until fresh, clean oil oozes out the top hole. Replace the top screw first; it will create an air lock that allows you to replace the bottom screw without the oil draining out.

2 Spray fogging oil into your carburetor(s) to remove condensation and prevent rust inside the engine. With the engine running in the water, fog the carburetor until the engine starts to smoke. Then detach the fuel line and let the engine run out of gas. Take the boat out of the water, lower the motor so the water drains out of the lower unit and turn the motor over a few times to blow out any remaining water.

3 Fill your gas tank at least halfway and then add fuel conditioner. This will prevent a buildup of gummy varnish that could clog your carburetor. Before running the boat in spring, top off your tank with fresh gas to dilute the conditioner and boost the octane level, which may decline over winter.

4 Remove the cowling and spray the entire engine with a light coating of silicone lubricant. This extends the life of the fuel line and other rubber or plastic parts. Be sure to inspect the fuel line for leaks.

5 Repack your boat trailer's wheel bearings. If water has seeped in, the bearings will rust over the winter. Inspect the races as well; if they're worn or pitted, replace them.

6 Check the fluid level in your batteries, add distilled water if necessary and bring the batteries to a full charge. Disconnect any electronics and store them inside. Unplug your trolling motors. Check the batteries a couple of times over the winter to make sure they're charged.

7 Tip up the bow and pull the plug so any water in the hull can drain out. If the water is not drained out, it will freeze and possibly damage the hull or floor.

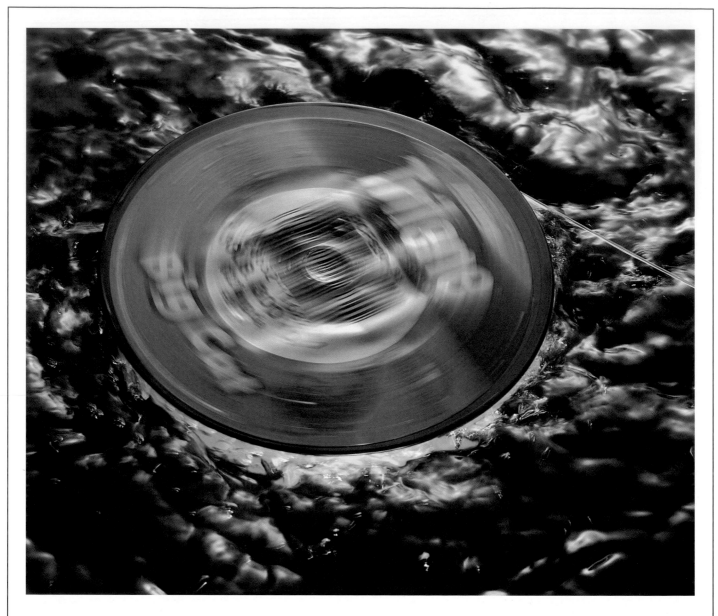

LINE TIPS

If you're confused about what kind of fishing line to use for what purpose, don't feel bad. So are millions of other anglers.

There is no single line that will fit every fishing application. The chart at right will help you select the right line for the type of fishing you're doing, and the pages that follow provide some additional tips for getting the best results from the various kinds of popular fishing lines.

Line-Selection Chart
(Ratings: 1=best, 5=worst)

LINE CHARACTERISTIC	TYPE OF LINE			
	Mono	Dacron	Superline	Fluorocarbon
Visibility	2	5	3	1
Castability	2	5	1	3
Water Resistance	3	5	1	3
Abrasion Resistance	2	1	5	2
Stiffness	3	2	1	5
Stretch	5	2	1	3
Knot Strength	1	1	4	5

Connecting Mono to Superline

Monofilament and superline are the two most common types of fishing line, and there will be times when you'll want to splice them together. In clear water, for example, you may want to add a monofilament leader to superline to reduce its visibility.

But the great difference in the diameter and stiffness of these materials makes splicing a challenge. If you try to use a blood knot, for example, it may slip or the thin superline will cut into the mono.

Either of the two knots shown here will do the job.

Both have a knot strength of 100 percent. These knots can also be used to splice superline to fluorocarbon and other lines of unequal diameter.

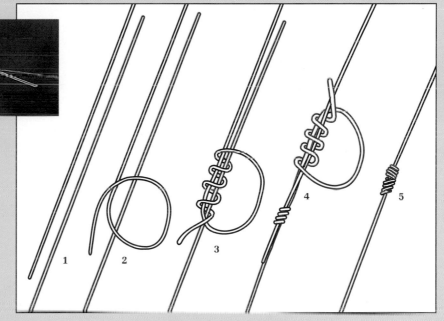

Double Uni-Knot. (1) Hold the two lines alongside each other, with the ends facing opposite directions; (2) form a loop with one of the lines, as shown; (3) pass the free end through the loop and around the standing line 4-5 times; (4) repeat steps 2 and 3 with the other line; (5) pull on both lines to draw the two knots together and snug them up.

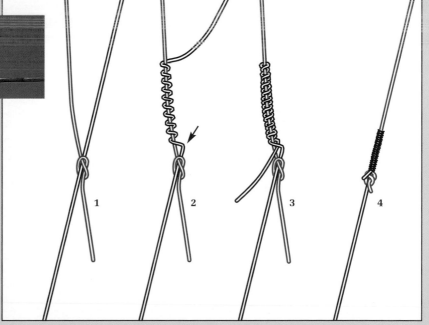

Spectra Knot. (1) Hold the lines end-to-end and then tie the mono around the superline using an overhand knot; (2) wrap the tag end of the superline around the mono about 10 times, leaving a small gap in the first wrap (arrow); (3) wrap the superline back over itself about 10 times and then push the tag end through the gap left in the first loop; (4) pull on both lines to snug up the knot (photo above), and closely trim the tag ends.

Stop Superline Slippage

Ever spool up your reel with superline only to find that you can pull line off the spool even when your drag is tightened to the max?

Before sending your reel in for repairs, try removing all the superline and adding a base of monofilament. Then attach the superline to the mono using a double uni-knot (p. 27).

More than likely, the slick superline was slipping on the spool, so tightening the drag did no good. Mono grips the spool much better and should solve the problem.

Cure Kinky Mono

Kinky or badly twisted mono is a real pain. Not only does it interfere with your casting, it wraps around your rod tip or reel handle at the most inopportune times.

One way to minimize line twist is to spool your line on properly in the first place. Different manufacturers wrap their line on the spool differently, so you may have to experiment to determine the spooling method that results in the least twisting.

But even if you do spool your line on the right way, kinks and twists are sure to develop as you're fishing, especially when you're vertically jigging or using lures that spin on the retrieve.

You could solve the problem by removing all your line and spooling on new line (below), but that's expensive and time consuming to do every time you get a kink; some other solutions are shown on page 29.

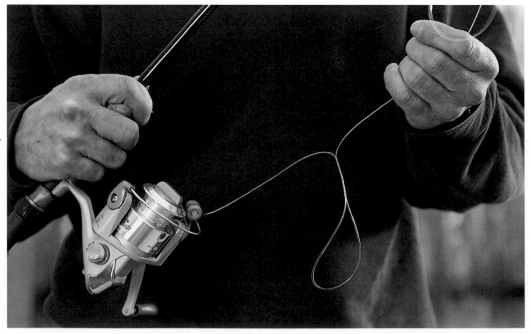

When spooling on new monofilament, test for line twist after adding a few dozen wraps (right). Pull some line off the reel spool and let it go limp; if it twists on its own, you're removing it from the wrong side of the spool. Try turning the spool over and removing the line from the other side and test for twist again. If the line is still twisting, put the spool on a nail and remove line from the end. Continue spooling with whatever method results in the least twist.

EFFECTIVE LINE-STRAIGHTENING METHODS

Pull & Stretch. To remove kinks, tie your mono to a tree or other solid object, then pull as hard as you can without snapping the line. Start stretching the line right at the tree and then continue stretching as you back away. For best results, stretch all of your line right down to the bare spool. Stretching will not solve severe line-twist problems, however.

Let It All Hang Out. To straighten badly twisted line, remove any lure or terminal tackle and then let the line out behind your boat. While motoring at high speed, let out all but a few wraps of line and pull it along for about half a mile. When you reel in, the twist will be gone.

False Cast. Untwist a short length of mono by removing the lure and then false casting the line, as you would if fly fishing. Six or eight false casts will usually do the job.

Knee Stretch. Straighten a mono leader by stretching it tight and then rubbing it rapidly across your knee. The friction heats up the line, realigning the molecules and removing the kinks.

LINE-SPOOLING TIPS

Easy Spooling Ideas. *When you want to remove line from the end of a spool but can't find a nail or screwdriver, try this: Lay the spool on carpet and reel with your rod tip right against the spool's lip (left). Or, if you're in your boat, just toss the spool into the water and start reeling (right).*

Maintain Tension. *Keep some tension on your line while spooling by holding it between your fingers as you reel (left). If you spool the line too loosely, a strong pull will cause the outer wraps to dig into the inner ones, resulting in a hopeless tangle (below).*

VALUABLE LINE TIPS

Barrel Swivel. When fishing with a lure that tends to twist your line, splice in a tiny barrel swivel 18 to 24 inches from the end. If you attach a bulky snap-swivel directly to the lure, it may interfere with the lure's action.

Criss-Cross. If you use a saltwater reel with no level wind, as many catfish and sturgeon anglers do, spool your line in criss-cross fashion by using your fingers to guide the line rapidly across the spool. This way, the bottom wraps prevent the top ones from digging into the spool when you hook a big fish.

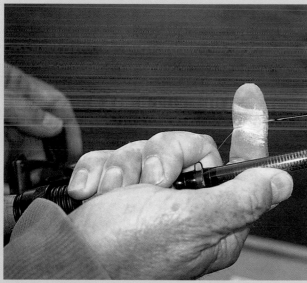

Reverse It. Superline tends to fray after heavy use, but that doesn't mean you have to replace the entire line. Just reverse the ends by winding the line onto another reel. Now the business end is brand new.

Use New Line. If you notice a buildup of a white, chalk-like powder on your fingers when spooling on mono, the line has probably started to deteriorate and weaken. To be on the safe side, remove the line and use a fresh spool.

ODDS 'N' ENDS

HANDY CRAWLER TOTE

When you're picking up nightcrawlers after dark, you're carrying a flashlight in one hand and grabbing worms with the other. That leaves no hands for lugging a worm box. Here's how to make a lightweight worm container that you can carry with a free finger:

Cut the top off a 1-gallon milk jug, leaving the handle intact as shown. Drop your worms into the opening; they won't be able to crawl back out.

NO-SLIP SPLIT-SHOT

If you've ever fished with a split-shot rig on a rocky or gravelly bottom, you know the problem: The shot hang up in the rocks and when you try to pull the rig free, the shot slide down to the hook (right). Your line soon gets frayed from sliding them back and you have to retie. Here are a couple solutions:

Use Some Teeth. Instead of using split-shot with a smooth groove (left), buy the kind with "teeth" in the groove to grip the line (right).

Loop Your Line. If you can't find shot with teeth, make a loop in your line and then pinch the shot onto the double line as shown. Pull on both ends to snug up the loop. Now the shot won't budge.

NIGHT-FISHING MARKER

It's difficult enough to follow structure during the day, and it's almost impossible when you're fishing after dark. You could place markers along the edge of the structure, but you'll need a spotlight to see them.

If you're a serious "night stalker," try this:

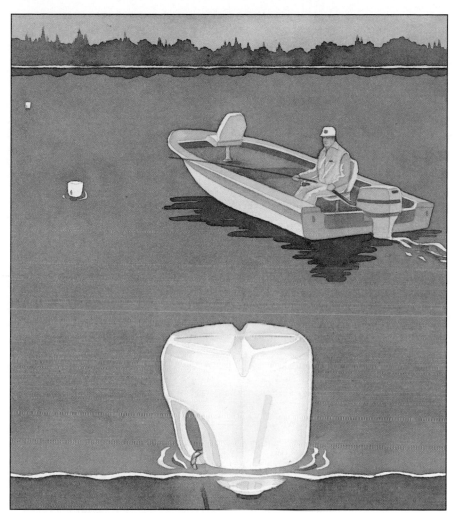

Glue a heavy sinker to the cap of a 1-gallon milk jug so it rides upside down. Then attach a cord and weight to the handle (left). When you're ready to use the marker, break a 6-inch Cyalume light stick and set it in the jug so it stands upright on the cap. By placing a line of markers along the edge of the structure, you'll have no trouble following the breakline (above).

SLIP-PROOF CRIMPS

The best way to attach terminal gear to braided-wire line, leader or downrigger cable is to use small metal crimping sleeves and a crimping tool. But if your crimp is not tight enough, the line could slip out and you'll lose your fish or your downrigger ball.

Here's how to attach the wire so it will never slip out of the crimp:

(1) Thread on a metal sleeve, (2) pass the end of the wire through a swivel or other terminal gear and then through the sleeve again, (3) pass the end through the sleeve a third time, (4) pull on the leader to draw the loop of wire into the sleeve and (5) firmly crimp the sleeve.

LONG-HANDLED NET BOOSTS SURVIVAL

Most anglers use a landing net with a short handle because it takes up less space in the boat. But many tournament anglers prefer nets with handles up to 8 feet long so they can reach a hard-fighting fish before it has a chance to throw the hook.

Besides improving your landing percentage, there's another good reason for using a long-handled net. By netting the fish sooner, you minimize the buildup of lactic acid in its blood, so the fish has a much better chance of survival should you choose to release it.

COATED MESH REDUCES TANGLES

When you hook a fish on a crankbait or other lure with treble hooks and scoop it up with an ordinary landing net, you can expect a major mess. The hooks poke through the weave of the netting material (inset) and when the fish flops, you wind up with a ball of netting with the fish in the middle. By the time you get the whole thing untangled, the fish is close to dead.

To avoid the problem, use a net with plastic-coated mesh. The hooks cannot penetrate the weave and, because the mesh is much stiffer, the fish cannot roll it into a tight ball.

Practical Fishing Tips

TRIM THE TUBE

Those inexpensive tube-style floats are great for slip-bobber fishing, but there's one problem. When you set the hook and miss, the sinker rams into the bottom of the tube and pushes it up too far, making the float list to the side (right). Here are two easy fixes:

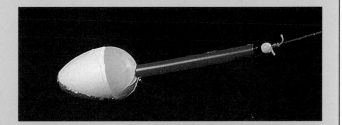

Trim It. *Remove the plastic insert at the top of the tube and trim both ends of the tube so they are flush with the float. Then replace the insert at the top of the tube so your stop does not slip through the float.*

Glue It. *Pull out the tube, smear a little glue on it and then push it back into place. Now the tube can't slip.*

STOP BOBBER-STOP HANG-UPS

Slip-bobber fishermen using spinning gear have a hard time casting because their line catches on the bobber stop (right). As the rig is sailing toward its target, the line stops suddenly and the bait tears off the hook. You can minimize the problem by keeping your spool full and using a gentle sidearm casting motion, but you'll still get some hang-ups. Here are two ways that veteran slip-bobber fishermen deal with the problem:

Method 1. *Leave your bobber stop untrimmed; this way, there are no stubby, stiff ends to catch your line. You can reel your line over the loose ends with no problem.*

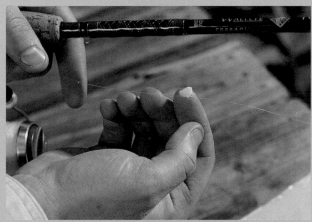

Method 2. *Trim the bobber stop closely and then coat it with beeswax. Now your line should slip right over the knot when you cast.*

EASY HOOK REMOVAL

If you're an avid angler, chances are you'll get a hook in your skin at some point in time. It could happen when trying to unhook a thrashing fish, or it may be the result of a careless cast by your fishing partner.

Human skin is incredibly tough and once a hook is sunk past the barb, it's very difficult to remove without further damage.

Here's a hook-removal trick used by many old-time fishing guides that could save you a trip to the doctor:

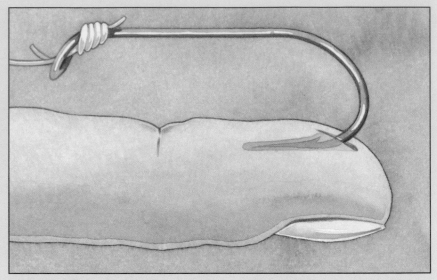

1 Always remove the hook from the same angle in which it entered the skin. Line up the hook so the shank is parallel to the long axis of the entry wound.

2 Make a secure loop in a length of mono (at least 20-pound test). Place the loop around the bend of the hook as shown. Then push the top of the hook toward the skin to open the wound slightly.

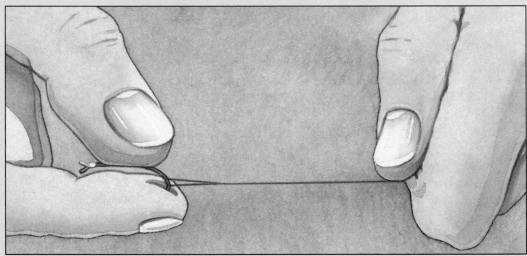

3 While maintaining downward pressure on the hook, give the mono a sharp jerk. Be sure the direction of pull is parallel to the long axis of the entry wound. The hook should pop right out.

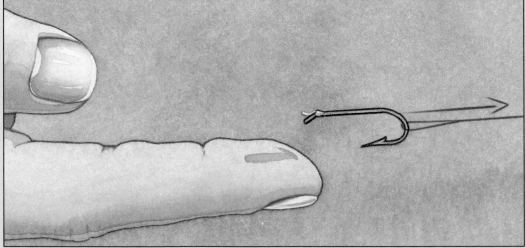

HANDY PLUG KNOCKER

Lots of crankbait fishermen carry some type of "plug knocker," which is a lead-bodied device intended to unsnag those expensive lures. Most plug knockers are attached to a heavy cord, but the cord always seems to be tangled when it's needed most.

Here's how you can rig your plug knocker so it's always available:

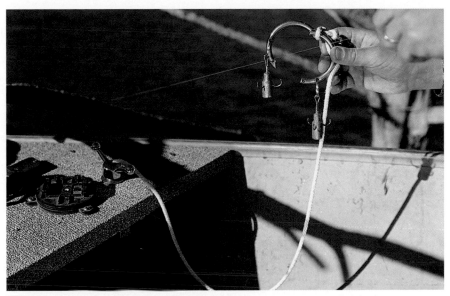

Tie your plug knocker to a retractable bow rope. When you get snagged, just clip the plug knocker onto your line, pull some rope out of the retractor and lower the device down to bump the lure free. Some models have dangling chains which catch the lure's hooks.

EMERGENCY LURE KNOCKERS

If your favorite lure gets snagged and you don't happen to have a plug knocker (above), don't give up and break off. Chances are you have something in your boat that will free the lure. Here are 3 common items that will do the job:

Clip On. Attach a clip-on sinker (at least 1 ounce) to your line, pull the line tight and then drop the sinker. It will slide down the line and bump the lure free. If desired, attach a piece of line to the sinker so you can retrieve it should you fail to free the lure.

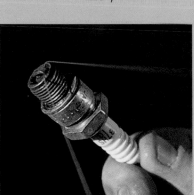

Spark Plug. Pinch an old spark plug over your line as shown; be sure the gap is completely closed so the line won't slip out. Then drop the spark plug to free the lure.

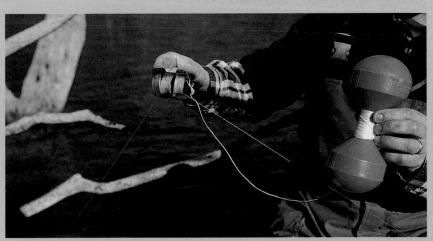

Strap Weight. Tightly wrap the strap weight from a marker buoy around your line, then strip some cord off the marker and drop the weight. It should free the lure.

BETTER NIGHT-LIGHT

Night fishermen know how important it is to have a good light in their boat. A strong light is a must not only for rigging, but for landing fish at boatside.

Most anglers carry a flashlight or a 12-volt spotlight. The only problem is, someone has to hold the light and the beam is too concentrated.

Here's how to make a light that will illuminate a large area—and it clips right onto the edge of your boat.

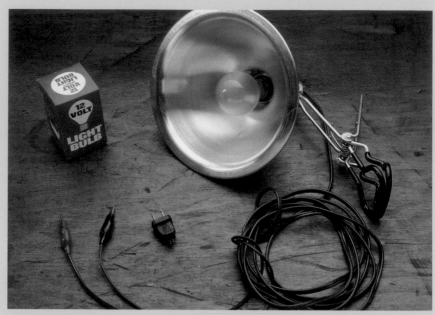

1 Replace the 110-volt bulb in an ordinary shoplight with a 12-volt bulb that fits into the socket. Then cut off the plug, split the wire and attach a pair of alligator clips. Attach the clips to your 12-volt boat battery.

2 Clamp the light to your boat's gunwale. You can then direct the light into the boat for rigging, or point it into the water alongside the boat for landing fish.

LONG LIVE THE MINNOWS

A minnow bucket with a perforated insert makes it easy to change water, and you can toss the insert into the lake and use it like a flow-through bucket. When you're moving around a lot, however, you probably don't want to keep hauling the insert in and out of the boat.

Unfortunately, the small bucket doesn't hold much water, so if you keep it in the boat, the minnows soon start to die from oxygen starvation.

Here's how you can keep your bait healthy considerably longer. The method also works well for keeping your bait alive at home.

Fill a 5-gallon pail with water and place the insert from your bucket inside the pail. The much greater volume of water keeps the minnows alive and the insert allows you to get at them easily.

NO MORE TANGLED LEADERS

Premade wire leaders save you a lot of time, but how do you store them without tangling? Most anglers just coil them up and wrap one end around the coils, but unless you unwrap them just right, you'll still wind up with a tangled mess.

There are two good ways to solve the problem:

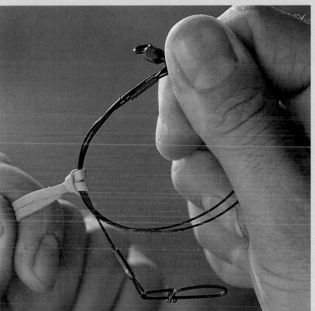

Rubber Band Loop. *Loop a thick rubber band around the coiled leader to secure the ends, then cinch the rubber band tight as shown. It won't come loose.*

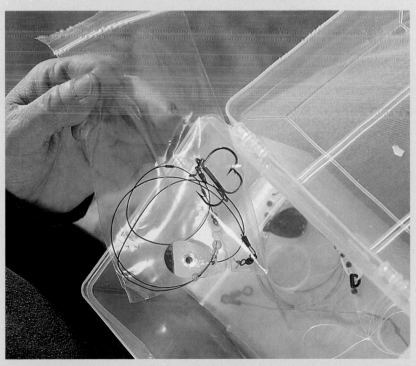

Resealable Bags. *Stuff the coiled leader into a small resealable plastic bag. Keep several leader bags in a small plastic box.*

MAP MAINTENANCE

Lake maps and river charts are indispensible fishing tools, but it's nearly impossible to keep them dry in a fishing boat. If they're not getting pelted with rain, they're soaking up windblown spray.

By using this 2-step process, however, your maps will last for years.

1 Brush your maps with a waterproof sealcoat like the kind you might use to seal your deck. Now the water won't soak into the paper.

2 Roll up your maps and store them in a plastic map pouch or map tube with watertight end caps. Or fold them and put them in a 1-gallon resealable plastic bag.

FOIL FLOAT FRUSTRATION

Those tall "cigar" floats are great for pike, catfish and other large gamefish, but stringing your line through them can be a real pain, especially when you're using superline or other highly flexible lines. The line hangs up inside the float and try as you may, you can't push it through.

Fortunately, there's a very simple solution:

Make a tight bend in the end of a piece of thin wire, push the wire through the bottom of the float and out the top, hook your line and pull it back through the float. The wire should be a permanent fixture in your tackle box.

SAVE SOFT PLASTICS

If you're like a lot of other anglers, you keep all of your soft plastics in a worm-proof plastic box. But over the course of the season, the colors get mixed up and, before you know it, your white grub tails are pink.

Here's how to prevent your soft plastics from bleeding, while keeping them soft and flexible:

Store each kind of soft plastic in a small, resealable plastic bag and don't combine colors. Add a few drops of worm oil to the bag to keep the baits soft and pliable.

"NET WEIGHT" METHOD AVOIDS INJURING FISH

It's nice to know the exact weight of a big fish you want to release, but hanging it on a scale often results in a serious injury to the fish. You have to poke the scale's hook into the jaw or gill arch and, should the fish start flopping, something's got to give.

You could solve the problem by buying a net with a built-in scale, or just weigh it as shown at right:

Leave the fish in the net, let most of the water drip off and then weigh the fish and the net as shown. After releasing the fish, weigh the net and then subtract that weight from the total weight to get the weight of the fish.

BASS TIPS

*T*ournament bass fishing has spawned an information bonanza as new techniques are devised and little-known secrets revealed.

LOOK FOR "INDICATOR" PLANTS

You're a lot more likely to find spawning bass on a firm sandy or gravelly bottom than on a soft, mucky one. But how do you know where to look when low water clarity prevents you from seeing the bottom?

Experienced anglers look for certain "indicator plants" to reveal what kind of bottom lies beneath them.

Typical hard-bottom plants include bulrushes (top left) and maidencane (top right). Typical soft-bottom plants include cattails (bottom left) and lily pads (bottom right).

WILD RICE REMEDY

In many north country lakes, wild rice makes prime summertime cover for large-mouths. But pulling a lure through the stringy weeds without fouling is nearly impossible.

Here's a simple way to fish a bed of wild rice without stopping after every cast to remove "salad" from your lure:

Retrieve your lure "with the grain" of the wild rice. The tops of the leaves should be pointing toward you, not away from you. Try to bring your lure through the slots in the vegetation.

WATCH THE SHADOWS

Given a choice, a bass will almost invariably select a shady resting spot. Whether you're fishing around standing timber, docks or steep cliff walls, you'll catch more bass by working the shady side of the cover rather than the sunny side.

But remember that the location of the shaded zone on the bottom is not necessarily directly below that on the surface, as the diagram at right shows.

Consider the angle of the sun when planning your casts. Try to visualize the location of the shaded zone on the bottom and be sure to cover the entire shaded area.

When a reservoir is drawn down in fall (top), the shallow structure is exposed and any weeds growing there die. When the lake fills again in spring (bottom), the shallow structure is flooded but still devoid of weeds, and the vegetation in deeper water remains.

RECOGNIZE REVERSE WEEDLINE

The weedline is a key location for bass because they can hide in the vegetation and dart out into the open to grab unsuspecting baitfish.

In natural lakes, the weedline forms at the depth where light penetration becomes insufficient for plant growth. Weeds are found only at that depth or *shallower*.

But some man-made lakes have a reverse weedline, meaning that weeds grow only at a certain depth or *deeper*. See why at left.

WILLOW-LEAF FOR WEEDS

A spinnerbait is one of the best lures for fishing in weeds because the safety-pin shaft runs interference for the hook and blade. Nevertheless, the blade may still foul in very dense vegetation.

Here's how to keep fouling problems to a minimum:

Select a spinnerbait with a willow-leaf rather than a Colorado blade. Because a willow-leaf blade spins at a smaller angle to the shaft than does a Colorado blade (inset), it is less likely to pick up bits of weeds and debris.

SMALL SQUIRT FOR SOFTER SKIRTS

The vinyl or rubber skirts used on spinnerbaits, Hula Poppers, jigs and other bass lures tend to stiffen up and lose action as they age. Eventually they mat up or become so brittle that some of the vinyl or rubber strips break off.

Here's how to add life to your skirts:

Periodically spray your vinyl or rubber skirts with ArmorAll Protectant. Treated this way, the skirts will stay pliable and retain their enticing wiggle indefinitely.

DOUBLE TRAILER

When you're fishing with a spinnerbait or buzzbait, short strikes are inevitable. The only way to catch these half-interested bass is to add a trailer hook. But with an ordinary single-hook trailer, you'll still miss plenty of fish.

Here's how you can put more of those short-strikers into your boat:

Push a treble hook over your main hook so the eye of the treble is level and the main hook is centered between the treble's two upper tines; clip off the bottom tine. Then remove the treble, slip a piece of surgical tubing over its shank so it covers the hook eye, and push the main hook through the tubing and eye of the treble. The double-hook trailer improves your odds of catching fish that strike short.

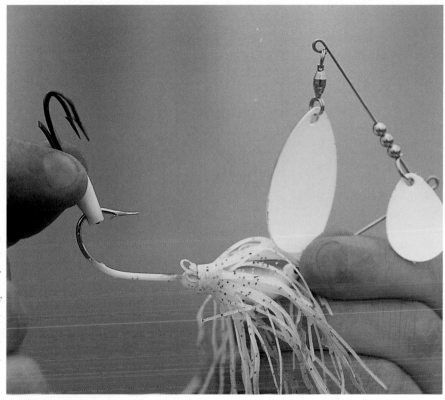

ADD THUMP TO SPINNERBAITS

A spinnerbait is one of the best lures for catching bass in murky water because the fish can easily home in on the vibrations of the blade.

But the thump of a willow-leaf blade is not as intense as that of a Colorado blade. Here's how you can add more thump to a willow-leaf spinnerbait:

Add a SuspenStrip (normally used for weighting minnowbaits) to one side of a willow-leaf blade. This throws the blade out of balance, intensifying the vibrations.

CURL BLADES FOR MORE BUZZ

Compared to most other topwaters, a buzzbait has a fairly subtle action. That makes it difficult for fish to see and track the lure in choppy water or after dark.

Here's how to modify buzzbait blades so they make a lot more commotion:

Roll the wings of a buzzblade around a ballpoint pen to bend them into a tight curl. The blades will catch more water and spit it in the air like a miniature Jet Ski.

TAILWEIGHTING TOPWATERS

Some topwaters, like stick-baits, have a built-in tail-weight; this way, the head rides high and the lure can be fished with a side-to-side "walk-the-dog" retrieve.

Other topwaters, such as propbaits and chuggers, can be fished with a walk-the-dog retrieve as well, but you must first add a little weight in the tail. Here's an easy way to do it:

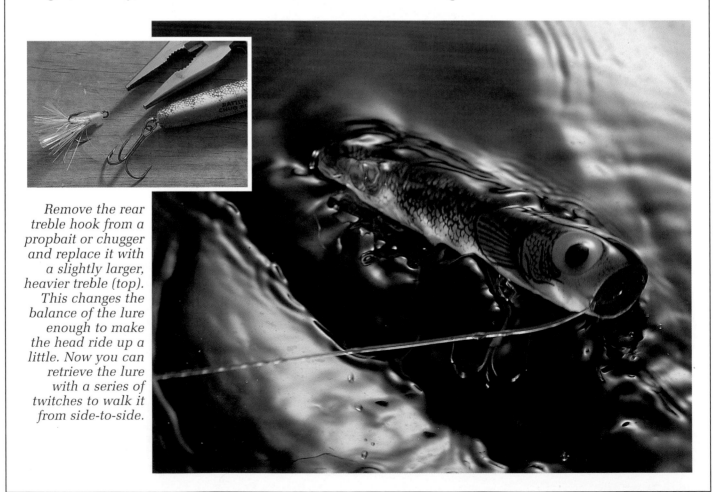

Remove the rear treble hook from a propbait or chugger and replace it with a slightly larger, heavier treble (top). This changes the balance of the lure enough to make the head ride up a little. Now you can retrieve the lure with a series of twitches to walk it from side-to-side.

PROPBAIT PLOYS

A twin-bladed propbait, such as a Smithwick Devil's Horse, is one of the best choices for luring bass out of heavy cover. The blades at either end of the lure make a lot of commotion, drawing the fish's attention.

In most cases, there is no need to modify the lure; it works just fine right out of the box. But serious propbait anglers have discovered three ways to make these lures work even better in certain circumstances:

Bend Blades Forward. When bass are finicky, try bending the prop blades forward (arrows). This way, the bait does not move forward as much when you give it a sharp twitch.

Reverse Propellers. In windy weather, reverse the front and rear propellers, hooks and attachment eyes. Then tie onto the rear eye. Now the lure has a more aerodynamic shape and will cast better in the wind.

Remove Front Propeller. To give the lure a walking action, remove the front propeller. This changes the lure's balance so the head rides higher.

ZIG-ZAG YOUR ZARA

Most bass pros consider a Zara Spook the best lure for "walking the dog." But some anglers have a hard time getting the hang of twitching the lure and then throwing slack into the line so it can glide to the side.

Here's a modification that makes it easier to achieve that enticing side-to-side action:

Remove the front screw eye and drill a hole halfway between that hole and the hole at the tip of the nose (left). Then reattach the screw eye in the middle hole (right). Now the lure will scoot from side-to-side more easily.

NOISY TUBEBAITS

Tubebaits are considered "finesse" lures; they're normally fished very slowly with minimal action. They work best in clear water where bass can get a good look at them. In discolored water, the fish may not detect a tubebait because it emits very little vibration.

If you're a tubebait fan, here are two ways of rigging these lures to make a little noise so bass can home in on them in even the darkest water.

Rattle Up Big Bass. *Rig your tubebait as you normally would, but push a piece of surgical tubing over the hook once the point is inside the tube. Then push a rattle into the surgical tubing and push the hook point through the other side of the tube.*

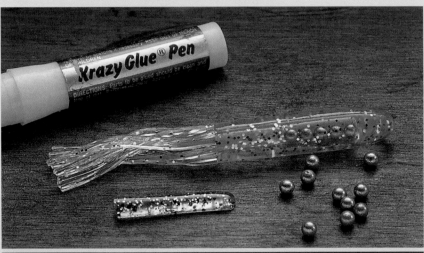

Steel Shot Trick. *Place a few steel shot in the nose of your tubebait, then super glue an inch-long piece of plastic worm inside the tube to hold the shot in place and create a "rattle chamber" (left). The shot also provide enough weight for a slow, gliding presentation.*

Using an offset worm hook, push the hook point into the nose of the worm and out the side so the nose rides neatly in the offset, then push the hook through the tube and the piece of plastic worm so the point penetrates the opposite side of the tube (bottom photo).

SPICE UP JIGGING SPOONS

A jigging spoon is nothing more than a chunk of heavy metal with a hook attached to it. Nevertheless, if you work it properly, it is one of the top deep-water bass lures.

Jigging spoons attract bass by the "dying bait-fish" action they have when jigged vertically. But bass in many waters see too many spoons and soon learn to avoid them.

Here's how to give your spoons a different look and a more seductive action:

Slip a tubebait over a thin-bodied jigging spoon, pushing the attachment eye of the spoon out the nose of the tube (left). Then fish the tube with a lift-and-drop action; the tentacles wiggle enticingly as the lure sinks, giving the spoon a realistic look.

A BETTER "FIZZING" BAIT

"Fizzing" is nothing new. For decades, anglers have poked small chunks of Alka-Seltzer into plastic worms or other soft-plastic lures so they emit bubbles that draw the attention of bass.

The problem is, the chunks sometimes fall out of the slits you cut in your lure. Here's a good way to prevent that from happening:

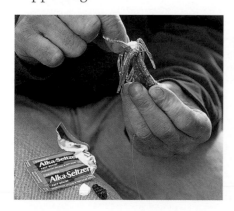

Cut a few small holes in a tubebait, insert some Alka-Seltzer chunks and then plug the tube with a piece of plastic worm (left). Now the chunks can't fall out and the fizzing lasts a little longer.

SHAKE UP STUBBORN BASS

One of the best ways to tempt strikes from post-spawn bass is to shake a plastic worm right in their face. With the worm on the bottom just in front of the bass, shake your rod tip rapidly to make the worm quiver without moving ahead.

While this method is effective, here's how to spice up your worm to draw even more strikes:

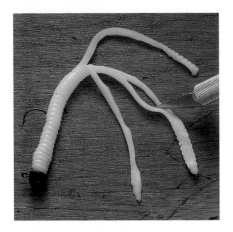

Using a razor blade or X-Acto knife, slice the back half of a floating worm lengthwise (left), then slice each half again to make 4 tentacles that will wiggle enticingly when you shake the rod tip (above). The worm can be Texas-rigged or fished on a mushroom jig with an open hook.

DOUBLE CAROLINA RIG

If you're into fishing with soft plastics, you probably use a Carolina rig at least part of the time. Because the rig employs a barrel swivel to keep the weight away from the hook, the lure settles more slowly than it would on a Texas rig, explaining why it often catches more bass.

Even though a Carolina rig ranks among the most effective methods for fishing soft plastics, pro bass anglers have found a way to improve the standard rig. Here's how they do it:

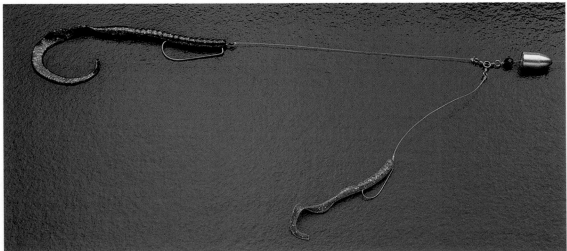

Substitute a 3-way swivel for the barrel swivel, then tie an 8-inch length of mono and a worm hook to the extra eye. Rig the second hook with a smaller soft plastic, such as a 4-inch worm.

WIELD A WACKY WORM

Another good way to catch fussy bass is to use a "wacky worm," which is nothing more than a plastic worm hooked through the middle. The worm is usually fished with no extra weight; this way, it sinks very slowly, giving lethargic bass plenty of time to grab it. And with the hook halfway back in the worm's body, you'll catch more short-strikers.

Here are the rigging details:

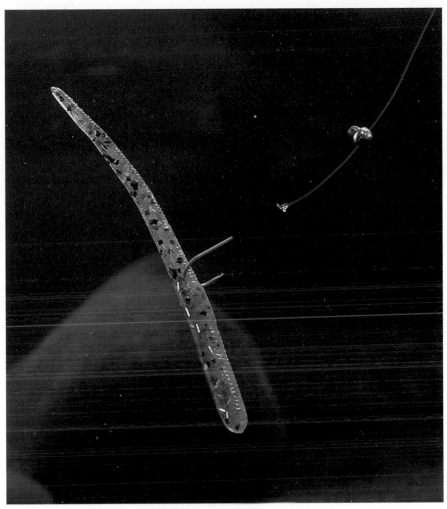

If you're fishing in light cover, push a straight hook through the middle of the worm, leaving the point exposed. In heavy cover, substitute a weedless hook. If you need a little more weight, add a small bullet sinker ahead of the hook, pinch on a split-shot a few inches up the line or push a finishing nail into the middle of the worm's body. Fish the worm on a light spinning outfit with 8-pound mono.

OFFSET JIG HOOK

Many live-bait hooks are offset, meaning that the hook point is bent away from the shank. This way, when a fish takes the bait and the hook is lying flat in its mouth, the point is more likely to catch in the upper or lower jaw on the hookset.

But very few bass jigs come with offset hooks. If you're missing too many fish, try this:

Using a needlenose pliers, bend the hook point to one side of the shank as shown. The offset need only be 5 to 10 degrees. If you try to bend the hook too far, it may break.

MIS-TUNE CRANKBAIT TO FISH DOCKS

When bass are tucked under docks, logs or other overhead cover, it's nearly impossible to get a lure into the "strike zone." If they're feeling aggressive, they'll dart out to grab a lure skirting the edge of the cover, but what if they're not in the mood?

All you need is a pair of pliers to solve the problem:

Slightly bend the eye of your crankbait in the direction in which you want the lure to track (below). To make the lure veer right, for example, bend the eye to the right. Then cast the lure as close to the dock as possible and reel steadily to bring the lure into the fish zone.

IN THE GROOVE FOR BASS

Some plugs, like minnow-baits and stickbaits, have better action if you tie your line to the lower portion of the attachment eye. But the line tends to slip up on the eye, and you have to keep sliding it back down. One way to minimize the slipping problem is to use a knot that employs a double wrap around the eye, such as a Trilene knot. But even that will eventually slip.

The tip at left shows you how to prevent your line from slipping—permanently.

File a shallow groove about midway down the lower half of the attachment eye. Tie on the lure and slip your line into the groove before snugging up the knot.

Yo-Yo Your Minnowbait

When you're sight fishing for shallow-water bass but they're paying no attention to the usual sight-fishing lures like tubebaits and worms, you need to try something different.

A floating minnowbait often works well because of its lifelike look and action, but the fish may ignore it if you reel it past them at normal speed.

Here's how you can yo-yo the lure right in their face until they strike out of sheer irritation:

Thread a ½- to ¾-ounce egg sinker onto your line before tying on a floating minnowbait. Retrieve the lure until it's right in front of the bass, then pause and let your line go slack so the lure floats up (left). Wait a few seconds and then tighten your line to pull the lure back down (right). You may have to yo-yo the lure for several minutes to irritate the fish into striking.

Easy Weighting Method

Neutrally buoyant minnowbaits are becoming more and more popular for bass fishing because they'll hang right in the face of the fish when you stop reeling. You can buy many neutrally buoyant models, but many anglers prefer to weight their favorite floating minnowbaits.

There are many ways to do the job, but this is the easiest method we've run across:

Attach a Luck "E" Strike Quik Clip weight to the front hook hanger of a floating minnowbait. Then toss the lure in the water; if it still floats, add a larger weight. If it sinks, use a smaller weight or trim off a little lead.

POP-OFF BALLOON

Anglers fishing for stripers and trophy largemouths often suspend a baitfish from a party balloon. The balloon rides very high in the water, so a lively shad or golden shiner can easily tow it around and cover a lot of water.

The balloon is normally tied around the line with an overhand knot. When a fish grabs the bait and runs, the balloon has to slide up the line, which creates a great deal of resistance and sometimes causes the fish to drop the bait.

Here's how to rig the balloon so that won't happen:

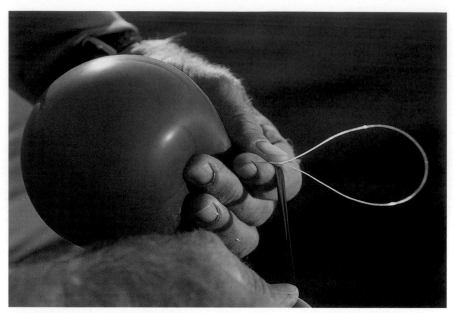

Make a loop in your line and tie the balloon around the doubled line using an overhand knot. Then, when a fish makes a run, it will pull the line out of the knot, freeing the balloon.

SPREADER RIG FOR STRIPERS

Stripers commonly feed by busting into huge schools of shad in open water. So it only makes sense that some imaginative anglers would come up with a rig that resembles a school of baitfish.

Here's how to make and use a "spreader" rig:

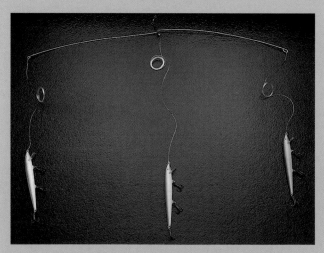

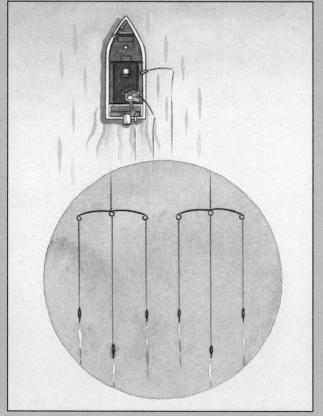

1 Bend an 18-inch piece of stiff wire as shown to make 3 attachment eyes. Tie a 30-inch mono leader (20-pound test) to each of the outside eyes and a 36-inch leader to the middle eye. Then attach 3 large minnowbaits or bucktail jigs tipped with curlytail grubs.

2 Clip your line onto the middle eye of the spreader rig and then troll it on either a flat line or a downrigger. Some anglers troll a pair of spreaders alongside each other to mimic a larger school of baitfish.

Practical Fishing Tips

FILE BARBS FOR PREFISHING

When prefishing before a tournament, you don't want to "burn" the fish you find. After catching a couple of fish on a spot, pull off and leave them alone until tournament time.

Some experienced tournament anglers take even greater pains to avoid messing up a good tournament spot.

File or pinch down the barbs of your hooks (left) before prefishing. When you hook a fish, fight it just long enough to determine its size, then let your line go slack and shake your rod tip to dislodge the hook. The fish will swim back to cover, none the worse for wear.

RECORD PREFISHING DETAILS

A serious tournament angler may check dozens of spots during a day of prefishing. However, it's nearly impossible to remember critical details about each spot. Some anglers carry a notepad to record the particulars, but taking notes is time consuming and difficult to do in windy or rainy weather.

Here's a much better way to keep track of the information you collect while prefishing:

Carry a small, hand-held tape recorder while prefishing. For each spot where you find bass, record details including landmarks, type of cover and structure, depth, time of day, weather conditions and lures used. When you get back home, plot in each spot on a lake map.

PANFISH TIPS

*T*here's a lot more to catching these scrappy fighters than dangling a worm beneath a float.

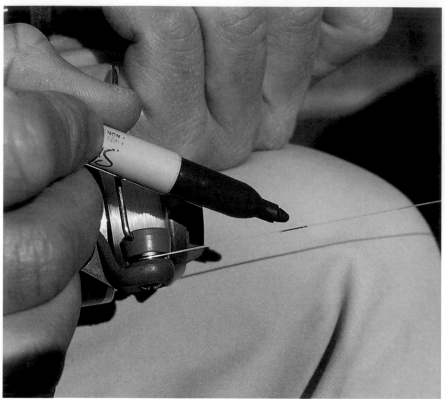

PINPOINT SUSPENDED CRAPPIES

Crappies are known for their habit of suspending in midwater. You can catch plenty of fish once you find that magic depth, but if you're not using a float, it's difficult to keep your bait or lure at the precise level. Here's a simple trick that solves the problem:

Measure the amount of line needed to reach the depth of the crappies and use a waterproof marker to color your line at that point. Then lower your bait until the colored mark reaches water level; it will be at exactly the right depth.

A LEVEL-HEADED JIG

Veteran crappie anglers know that a jig hanging level looks more natural and catches more fish than one hanging vertically. To make your jig hang level, you must secure your knot in the middle of the attachment eye (right). But an ordinary knot slips easily and you have to constantly reposition it. Here's a special knot that will keep your jig riding level:

(1) Pass your line through the hook eye 3 times, leaving 3 loose loops; (2) wrap the tag end around the standing line 5 times; (3) push the tag end through the 3 loops; (4) snug up the knot and position it in the middle of the hook eye as shown.

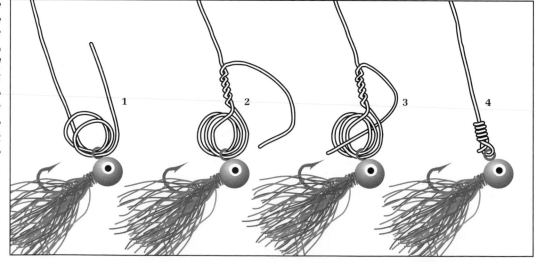

Practical Fishing Tips

ICE FISHING IN SUMMER

Ice fishermen catch plenty of crappies, perch and white bass on lead-bodied "swimming minnow" lures, such as the Jigging Rapala. But for some reason, few anglers think of trying these lures in open water.

Next time you locate a school of minnow-eating panfish, try working a swimming minnow just as you would if you were ice fishing. You'll be amazed at the results.

Lower a swimming minnow (size 2 or 3) vertically, keeping it just above the school. Twitch your rod to make the lure glide to the side and then hold your rod tip still as the lure settles to rest. The fish usually strike when the lure stops moving.

DROP IN ON CRAPPIES

A tiny jig ($\frac{1}{64}$ to $\frac{1}{80}$ ounce) is a dynamite crappie lure, but it's too light to cast with most tackle and it won't stay down if you try to troll with it. You could fish it beneath a float, but then you won't be able to cover much water.

Here's a unique dropper rig that enables you to cover lots of water with these minuscule lures—and you could catch some larger gamefish while you're at it.

Tie a 12- to 16-inch length of 6-pound mono to the rear hook of a 6- to 7-inch minnowbait, and then attach the tiny jig. When you troll slowly, the minnowbait draws the attention of crappies; when they move in for a closer look, they spot the jig and hit.

SLIP-FLOAT SAVVY

Practically everything you read about panfishing these days involves going light: ultralight rods, micro lures and tiny floats. But going super-light is not a good idea when you're fishing in the wind with a slip-float.

A tiny float requires a tiny weight for balance, and that tiny weight may not be sufficient to pull your line through the float when the wind is howling. The result: Your bait never makes it to the depth of the fish.

The solution is to use a larger float and weight it heavily so it takes only a slight tug to pull it under.

With a lightly weighted float (left), the wind catches your line and prevents the weight from pulling it down to the stop (arrow). With a larger float and heavier weight (right), the stop is drawn all the way to the float so your bait can reach the proper depth.

RESEARCH UNTAPPED TREASURES

Good-sized panfish are getting harder and harder to find, but there are still some waters that have them—if you you don't mind doing a little research.

Panfish are not particularly net-shy, so they can be accurately sampled with test nets. Consequently, lake-survey reports available from natural-resource agencies are a good reflection of what's in the lake. At right is a sample report and how to interpret it.

Length of Selected Species Sampled

Number of fish netted for the following length categories (inches)

Species	0-5	6-8	9-11	12-14	15-19	20-24	25-29	>30	Total
Black Bullhead	–	1	–	19	–	–	–	–	20
Black Crappie	31	106	58	31	–	–	–	–	226
Bluegill	128	186	47	29	–	–	–	–	390
Brown Bullhead	–	–	–	33	16	–	–	–	49
Green Sunfish	41	21	10	–	–	–	–	–	72
Hybrid Sunfish	7	25	–	–	–	–	–	–	32
Largemouth Bass	1	85	7	10	2	–	–	–	105
Muskellunge	–	–	–	–	–	–	1	–	1
Northern Pike	–	–	–	–	5	35	28	7	75
Pumpkinseed	40	71	17	–	–	–	–	–	128
Rock Bass	10	87	32	28	–	–	–	–	157
Smallmouth Bass	–	24	74	72	17	–	–	–	187
Walleye	–	11	30	14	34	60	7	–	156
Yellow Bullhead	–	1	39	114	–	–	–	–	154
Yellow Perch	21	153	59	41	–	–	–	–	274

Check the length-frequency distribution on a survey report (circled data) to determine a lake's trophy panfish potential. For example, try to find waters that have a fair number of bluegills over 9 inches and crappies over 11 inches in length.

KEEP YOUR DISTANCE

When sight fishing for spawning panfish in clear water, you must dangle your bait right in their face. But with an ordinary spinning rod, you'd have to get your boat so close to the fish that you'd spook them. You could use a cane pole or extension pole, but they tend to be clumsy and lack sensitivity. Here's a better solution:

Attach your spinning reel to an 8½- to 9-foot fly rod. This way, you can place your bait right in front of the fish without spooking them, and you can cast if necessary.

SUBTLE MARKER

If you spot some bedding panfish in bulrushes or other emergent weeds, but they spook before you can get your bait into the water, you'll have to mark the spot and come back later. But if you use an ordinary marker buoy, someone else is likely to see it and beat you to the punch.

Here's how to mark the spot so only you will be able to find it:

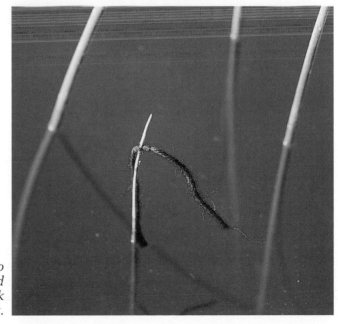

Tie a piece of yarn around a weed stem right next to the bedding area. Then wait 15 or 20 minutes and approach quietly. Chances are, the fish will be back in exactly the same spot.

Double Duty for 'Gills

Bluegills love tiny fly-rod poppers—when the water is warm and calm and they're in the right mood. But when the conditions aren't right, they're more likely to take a subsurface fly. Here's a unique rig that allows you to cover both fronts:

Tie a 2-foot length of 4-pound mono to the bend of the popper's hook and then attach a tiny nymph or wet fly (size 10 or 12). Sometimes the fish prefer the popper; other times, the fly. When they're hitting the fly, the popper serves as a strike indicator.

Worm Wisdom

When fishing panfish with worms, the standard wisdom is that you must hide your hook point so the fish won't "see it." But that only serves to cut down your hooking percentage. You'll have better luck if you leave the point exposed. The fish don't mind at all.

Another common mistake is threading the worm all the way onto the hook so the fish can't steal your bait. The problem is, they may not hit the lifeless offering.

The photos below show the wrong way and the right way to hook worms for panfish:

Wrong. *Worm threaded completely onto the hook with no end dangling; hook point covered.*

Right. *Worm hooked several times with end left dangling; hook point exposed.*

DEEP-BASIN CRAPPIES

When you're fishing a shallow to medium-deep lake in late fall or winter and don't have a clue as to where the crappies might be, try this:

Examine a hydrographic map of the lake and find the deepest hole (arrow). Then scout it thoroughly with your depth finder. The fish could be anywhere from the middle depth to just off the bottom.

GENERATE BETTER CRAPPIE RESULTS

It's a well-known fact that lights draw crappies at night, but some southern anglers have taken the concept to the extreme by equipping their boats with a small generator and a bank of 110-volt floodlights. The vibration from the generator also helps draw fish to the boat. (Be sure to check your state's regulations before trying this method.) Here's how the system works:

Mount 110-volt halogen floodlights around the gunwales, and plug them into the generator. Double-anchor your boat to keep it in the same spot, let the generator run for at least 20 minutes to attract crappies. Then scatter minnows on slip-bobber rigs through the lighted area. Experiment to find the most productive depth.

SPEED UP FOR WHITES

Jigs are an excellent choice for pack-feeding white bass; with their single hook, you can unhook the fish in a hurry and get back into the water while the action is still hot. But some anglers have trouble catching pack-feeders on jigs because they work them much too slowly. Here's the key to improving your jig fishing success:

Cast just past the feeding pack and then begin your retrieve as soon as the jig hits the water. Hold your rod tip high and reel fast enough to keep the lure above the fish (red line). If you let the jig sink and work it slowly, as you would for most other fish (blue line), whites will usually ignore it.

PROVOKE A PERCH FRENZY

When you find a school of aggressive yellow perch and start catching them one after the other, the activity often draws even more perch, starting an intense feeding frenzy. If you take a break and stop catching fish, however, the activity slows down in a hurry. Here's how to keep the action hot and heavy:

When you're fishing with a partner, try to keep one line in the water at all times. If you both take a break, get your lines tangled or spend too much time getting fish off the hook, the school may disperse.

ACTIVATE LETHARGIC LEECHES

Small leeches are a top-notch bait for sunfish, perch and other panfish. But in order to keep them alive for a long period of time, they must be held at a temperature of 50°F or less. At that temperature, however, they lose their enticing wiggle and may even ball up around your hook, so the panfish ignore them.

Here's how to activate your leeches and restore their wiggle without endangering your entire supply:

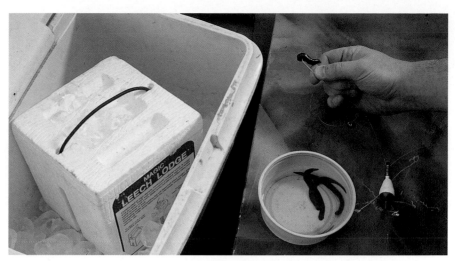

Keep your leech bucket in a cooler with plenty of ice and take out only a few at a time. Place them in a small container and let them warm in the sun for several minutes before using them. They'll start swimming the second they hit the water. Use the same method when using larger leeches for walleyes, smallmouth bass, etc.

DON'T LET PANFISH STUMP YOU

Submerged stumps are hot-spots for crappies and sunfish, but there's a lot more to fishing a stump than tossing a bait next to it and waiting for something to happen. The main reason stumps attract so many fish is that they have numerous nooks and crannies in which the fish can hide (inset).

If you soak a minnow on one side of the stump, crap-pies hiding in crevices on the other side may not even see it.

Veteran stump fishermen work a typical stump as shown below:

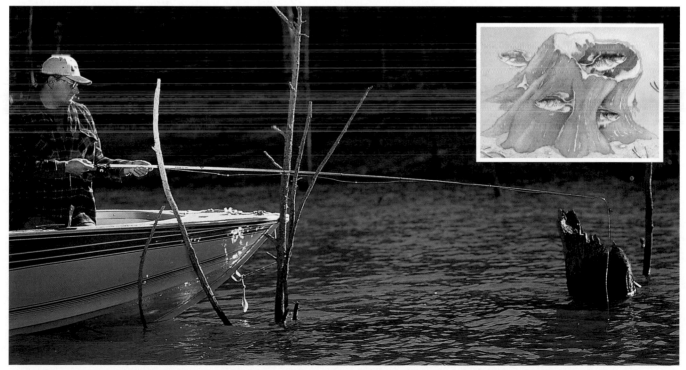

Position your boat so your shadow does not fall across the stump. Use an extension pole or cane pole to dip a minnow around the entire perimeter of the stump and even into the rotted-out opening in the center. The inset shows panfish using a submerged stump.

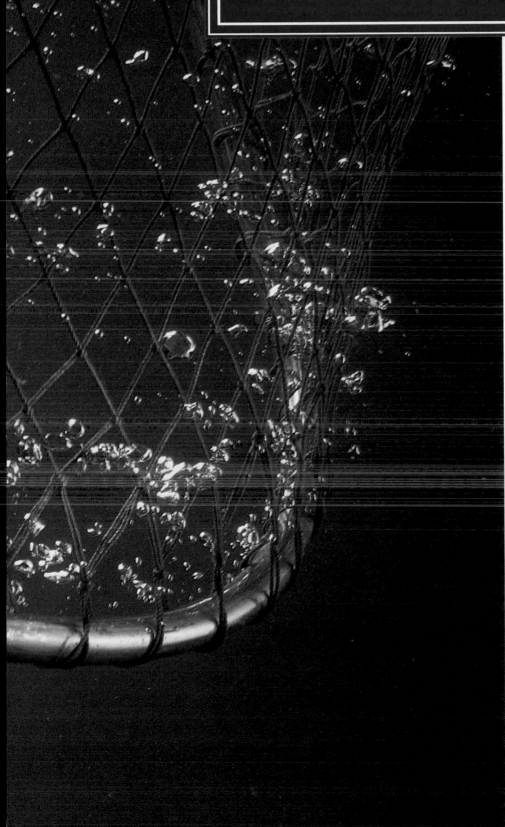

WALLEYE TIPS

*W*hen these elusive gamefish decide not to bite, you'll need every trick in the book to change their minds.

TWO-WAY THREE-WAY

Lots of walleye anglers rely on 3-way swivel rigs to fish baits and lures in deep water. An ordinary 3-way rig (below) consists of a 3-way swivel with the main line tied to one eye, a dropper and heavy sinker to another eye and a leader with a bait or lure to the remaining eye.

At right is a 3-way rig that will catch even more walleyes.

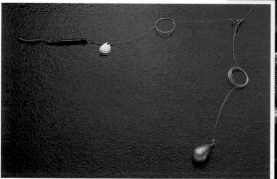

Standard 3-way swivel rig.

An even better idea: Substitute a heavy jig for the sinker on your 3-way rig. This way, you can catch walleyes on the bait or lure and on the jig.

SLOWER SINK RATE

When you hear walleye experts discussing the finer points of jig fishing, they'll invariably mention sink rate. The idea is to select the slowest-sinking jig that will still get you to the bottom, taking wind and current into consideration. Walleyes almost always grab a jig on the drop, and the slower it sinks, the more strikes you'll get because the fish have more time to make their decision.

You can reduce the sink rate simply by using a lighter jig head or heavier line, either of which has more water resistance. Here's another suggestion:

Add a bulkier trailer. If you're fishing with a jig tipped with a 3-inch curlytail grub (top), for example, replace it with a 4-inch (bottom). Or, if you're using a plain jig head tipped with a minnow, try a feather or bucktail jig with a minnow.

ODD-SIZED JIG HEADS

In many jig-fishing situations, a sixteenth of an ounce makes a huge difference in how fast your jig sinks. But most jig manufacturers only offer jigs in multiples of an eighth ounce. In other words, you can buy jigs weighing $1/8$, $1/4$, $3/8$, $1/2$ ounce, etc., but you'll seldom find the in-between sizes of $3/16$, $5/16$ and $7/16$ ounce.

Here are several ways to solve the problem:

Make Your Own. *Buy a mold that has a selection of head sizes including the in-between sizes that you want. You may have to buy more than one mold to get all the sizes you need.*

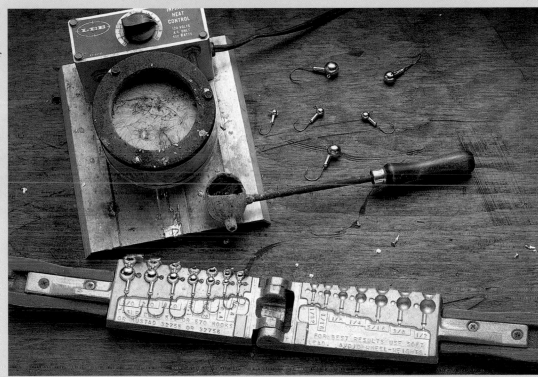

Look for Oddballs. *If you buy a lot of jigs, you've probably noticed that there's a lot of variation in weight from one manufacturer to another. To determine the precise weight of a certain jig, weigh it on a precise scale. It may just be the odd size you're looking for.*

Try Tin. *Try molding your jig heads out of tin rather than lead. A tin jig head weighs only about 60 percent as much as a lead-head of the same size, so it will sink much slower yet have a larger profile than a lead-head of the same weight.*

STAND-OUT STINGER

A jig and minnow combo is a top-rate walleye bait but, when the fish are fussy, they grab the tail of the minnow and not the hook. Some anglers surprise these short-strikers by tying a "stinger" (a small treble hook) to the bend of their jig hook using a short length of mono.

But a stinger hook tied on this way tends to droop below the jig and may not be in the right position when a walleye strikes. And if you stick the treble into the min-now, it interferes with the action, resulting in fewer strikes.

Here's how to make the stinger stand out straight so it trails right next to the min-now's tail:

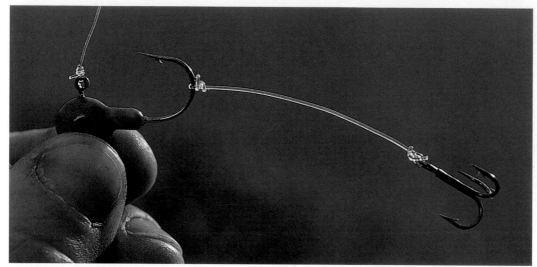

Attach a size 12 treble hook to the bend of your jig hook using a piece of 15-pound-test hard mono (the type used to make fly-leader butts). Tie the mono onto the jig hook using a double-clinch knot; the double wrap holds the line in the right position.

STOP BITE-OFFS

When you're jig fishing for walleyes in waters with lots of northern pike, you'd better have a good supply of jigs. With the line tied directly to your jig head, a pike will snip off your jig in a heartbeat.

You could clip your jig onto a braided-wire leader but that will cut down on the number of walleye bites.

Here's how you can prevent bite-offs while still catching walleyes and some "bonus" pike:

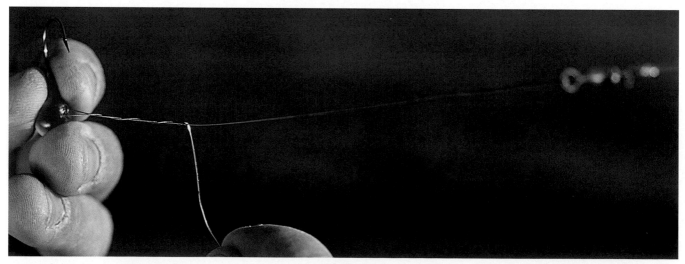

Using haywire twists, attach a 6-inch length of stainless-steel wire (20-pound test) to your jig and to a small barrel swivel. Then tie the swivel to your line. The thin wire won't reduce the number of walleye bites and you'll catch the pike rather than letting them bite you off.

FINER POINTS OF JIG SELECTION

There's a lot more to choosing a jig head than picking the right weight and color. You also have to consider hook size and "gap," meaning the distance between the top of the eye and the hook point (below). If the hook is too small for the size of the jig head, or the gap too narrow, you'll miss more fish than you hook.

When tipping your jig with a minnow or soft-plastic trailer, use a jig head with a relatively large hook (top). If the hook is too small (bottom), the minnow or trailer fills the gap, reducing your chances of hooking a fish.

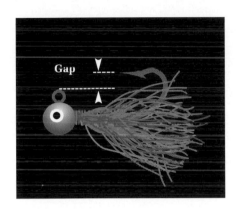

Gap

A narrow gap is an even bigger problem if your hook has a short shank. It's easy to see why this long-shank jig hook (top) would hook more fish than the short-shank hook (bottom), even though the gap is identical.

WHEN IN DOUBT —SET THE HOOK!

Don't expect to feel a sharp tug when a walleye takes your jig. In trying to describe how a strike feels, you'll hear experts use terms like "tic," "tap," "bump" and "nudge." And sometimes you feel nothing at all—the jig just stops moving or doesn't sink the way it should.

The best policy is to set the hook immediately whenever you feel anything out of the ordinary. Here's why:

A walleye "inhales" a jig by flaring its gills and sucking in a volume of water (including the jig). If you don't set the hook immediately, it will blow the jig out just as quickly.

WATCH THE BIRDY

Experienced walleye fishermen are faithful bird watchers. They know that fish-eating birds are good indicators of baitfish concentrations that often reveal the presence of walleyes.

Most anglers know that gulls and terns often pinpoint schools of baitfish, but other kinds of birds are worth watching as well.

Shallow-Water Birds. *When walleyes are feeding in the shallows, herons, egrets and other fish-eating wading birds will help you find schools of baitfish that attract walleyes.*

Deep-Water Divers. *When walleyes are feeding on deep structure, loons, cormorants and other diving birds not only show you where the baitfish are, they often reveal the location of humps, saddles and other deep structure that may otherwise be difficult to find.*

Pay Attention to Turnover

The fall turnover usually means tough walleye fishing. Because the water mixes thoroughly, the temperature is the same from top to bottom and the fish can be just about anywhere.

But the turnover occurs at different times in different lakes depending on factors such as latitude and depth.

Here are some clues that will help you determine when your lake is turning over:

Look for "Gunk." *Globs of organic "gunk" often break loose from the bottom and float to the surface when a lake is turning over. You'll often see the greenish or brownish globs and you may even notice a reduction in water clarity, or a faint smell similar to rotten eggs.*

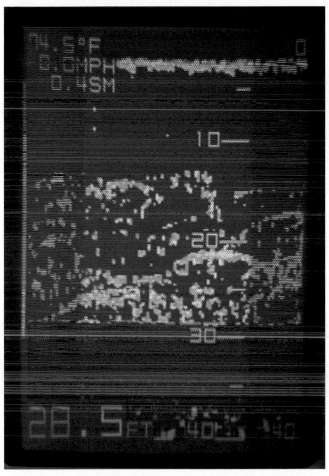

Graph It. *If your graph is showing baitfish and plankton scattered at all depths, the lake is probably turning over. Sometimes you'll see larger marks indicating walleyes mixed in with the baitfish.*

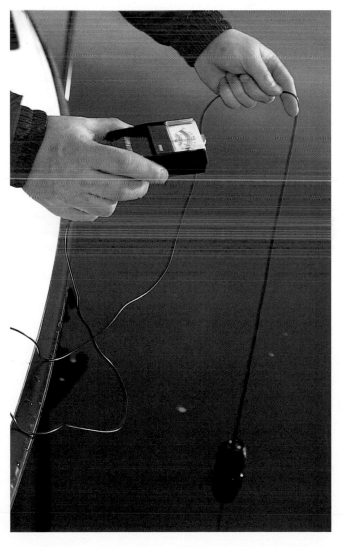

Probe the Temperature. *The only sure way to know when a lake is turning over is to lower a temperature probe. If the water temperature is within a degree or two from top to bottom, turnover is in progress. After turnover, the bottom temperature will be a few degrees warmer than the surface temperature, and the fish will be in deep water.*

WING-DAM WISDOM

If you're a big-river walleye fisherman, you probably spend some time fishing wing dams, those man-made rock structures that divert current toward the middle of the river.

But not all wing dams are created equal. Shown below are the elements of a good wing dam versus a poor one, and on the following page are some subtle wing-dam features that concentrate walleyes:

Good Wing Dam Vs. Poor Wing Dam

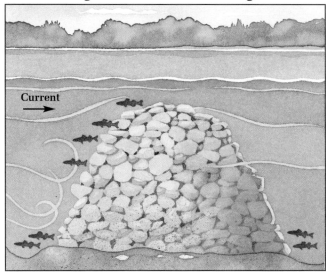

Good Wing Dam. *The best wing dams have plenty of clean rock, a wide top that serves as a feeding area and deep water on both the upstream and downstream sides that provides resting areas.*

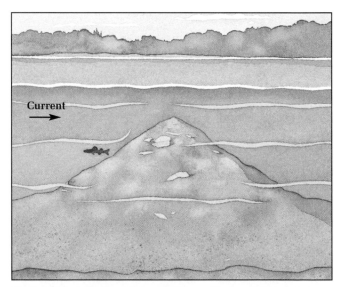

Poor Wing Dam. *Most of the rocks are silted over, the top is quite narrow and the water above and below the wing dam is relatively shallow. This wing dam does not provide a suitable feeding or resting area for walleyes.*

SUBTLE WING-DAM FEATURES

Jogs. *Not all wing dams are perfectly straight; on some, the upstream lip has a jog or indentation that attracts walleyes. Once you find one of these inside turns, carefully note its location; chances are it will always hold a few fish.*

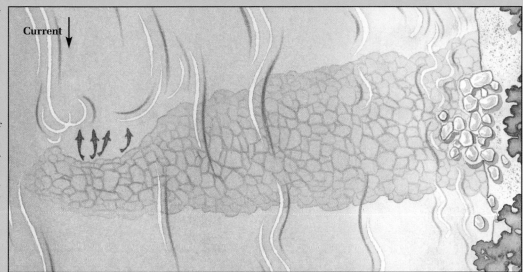

Slots. *Just as the upstream lip of a wing dam is not always straight, neither is the top of the wing dam. Certain wing dams have a low spot or "slot" that acts as a funnel. Slots make excellent feeding stations, and walleyes commonly line up along their edges.*

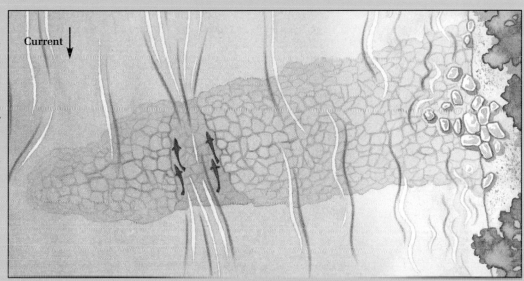

Sweet Spot. *The current speed varies considerably over the length of a typical wing dam. As a rule, the current is slowest near shore and fastest near the main river channel. Walleyes favor a moderate current, so the secret is to find the "sweet spot" where the current is just right.*

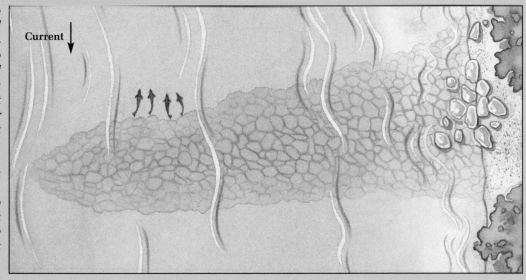

ADJUSTABLE DROPPER RIGS

Walleye anglers use dropper rigs for a variety of live-bait and artificial-lure presentations. A dropper rig helps you keep your bait or lure just the right distance off bottom to avoid snagging in rocks or wood, or fouling in weeds or algae.

One problem with a dropper rig is that you don't always know how long the dropper should be, so you have to experiment by tying on dropper lines of different lengths. And you may have to experiment with leader length as well. Yet another problem: The sinker is bound to get snagged, and you could lose the entire rig.

Here are some dropper rigs that will solve each of these problems:

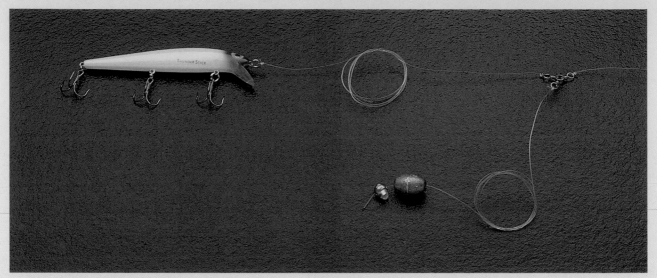

Adjustable 3-Way Rig. *Attach your main line, a long dropper and a leader to a 3-way swivel, then thread an egg sinker onto the dropper and pinch on a split-shot to secure the egg sinker. Now you can adjust the length of the dropper by sliding the split-shot one way or the other. And should the sinker get snagged, a strong pull will slide the split-shot off the dropper. You lose the sinker and shot but save the rest of the rig.*

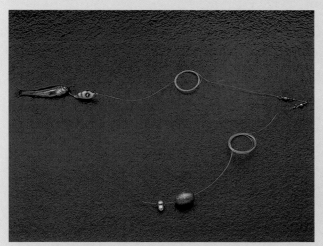

Adjustable Slip Rig. *Tie a long dropper to a barrel swivel, thread the swivel onto your main line, then attach your line and leader with another barrel swivel. Add an egg sinker and split-shot to the dropper. This makes an excellent live-bait rig because a fish can take line without dragging the sinker, and you adjust the length of the dropper.*

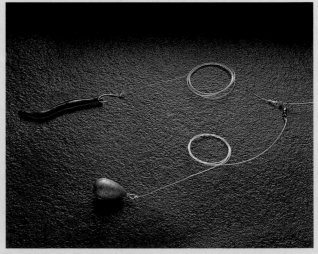

Adjust Everything Rig. *The only difference between this rig and the adjustable slip rig (left) is that you substitute a sliding stop and bead for the barrel swivel connecting the line and leader. This enables you to adjust not only the length of the dropper but the length of the leader as well.*

LIGHT UP YOUR SIDE PLANERS

Trolling with side planers is a great way to catch walleyes when they move into the shallows in the evening. The boards pull your lures to the side of the boat where the walleyes won't be spooked.

But once it gets dark, the boards are difficult to see and you can't tell how far they are from shore.

Rather than fishing blind and possibly running one of your boards into a tree, stick-up or another boat, try this:

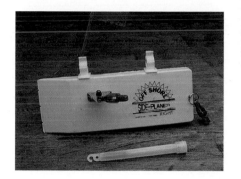

Screw a pair of metal clips to the top of your side planer (left) and insert a Cyalume light stick. Now your planers are easy to see and will light up the surrounding area enough that you'll be able to see tree branches and other obstacles.

IN THE SHADE OF THE MOON

Most walleye night stalkers like to fish during the full moon. Not only do the fish seem to feed more heavily when the moon is full, it's a lot easier to see what you're doing.

But some die-hard night fishermen have noticed a pattern that helps them catch even more walleyes, especially the bigger ones:

When fishing under a full moon, look for areas that are shaded from the moon's rays. You might find the fish near steep banks, along shorelines with tall trees or under bridges.

A Touch of Color

When you're fishing with a live-bait rig, a natural presentation normally works best—a sinker, a plain hook and the bait— with no frills or fancy stuff.

But when the fish are finicky, there are times when a little color or flash helps get their attention and bring them in.

Here are three ways to trigger a few more bites from fussy walleyes:

Bit of Yarn. *Begin tying a Trilene knot. After making the double loop through the hook eye, insert a piece of colored yarn from 1 to 1½ inches long into the double loop and then finish the knot as you normally would. After snugging up the knot, pull the yarn back to cover the hook.*

Bead or Corkie. *Thread a colored plastic bead or a Corkie (round Styrofoam float used for steelhead fishing) onto your leader before tying on your hook. A Corkie not only adds color, it has enough flotation to keep your bait slightly off the bottom.*

Flicker Blade. *Thread on a clevis with a size 0 Colorado blade, add a few colored beads and then tie on your hook. Make sure the convex side of the blade is facing the hook.*

TANDEM-HOOK CRAWLER RIG

Nightcrawlers rank among the deadliest of walleye baits. For a natural presentation, all you have to do is hook the worm through the nose with a small single hook.

But with the worm hooked this way, the fish have an annoying habit of striking short, leaving you with only half of your bait.

If you're tired of "feeding the fish," try this tandem-hook rig:

1 Thread a size 6 bait hook with a turned-up eye about 8 inches up your leader (8-pound mono), (2) make a loop over the hook as shown, (3) wrap the end of the leader through the loop about 5 times, (4) snug up the knot by pulling on both ends of the leader and (5) tie a size 6 straight-eye bait hook to the end of the leader so it's about 3 inches from the other hook.

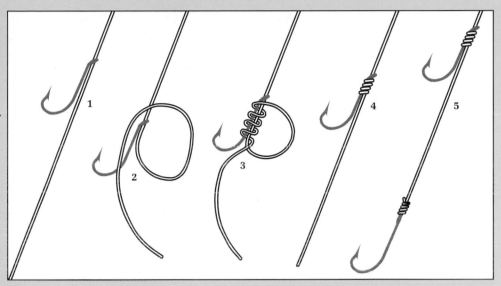

2 Push the first hook through the head of the crawler and the second hook through the middle of the body. The worm should hang straight, with no kinks or coils of loose line.

3 When you feel a pick up, set the hook immediately rather than feeding line as you would with a single-hook rig. Much of the time, the fish will be caught on the rear hook.

PIKE & MUSKIE TIPS

*P*ike & muskie specialists have an enormous trick bag that helps them outwit these powerful fighters.

FOIL FOLLOWERS

Muskies and, to a lesser extent, pike, have an aggravating habit of following a lure right up to the boat and then turning away at the last instant.

Most anglers know that they can draw strikes from some of these followers by plunging their rod tip into the water and sweeping their lure in wide figure-8s.

The tips here show some other ways that pike/muskie experts convince followers to grab their lures:

Cross Paths. When fishing with a partner, plan your casts so the paths of your lures cross several feet before they reach the boat. This way, a fish following one lure spots the other lure veering off at an angle, and the threat of its prey escaping often prompts a "reaction" strike.

Go Back with Bait. *Set up another rod with a sucker or other large baitfish on a quick-strike rig and keep the baitfish in a bucket so it's ready to use (above). Then, should a fish follow your lure but refuse to strike, mark the spot and leave it alone for 15 or 20 minutes. When you return, toss out your quick-strike rig and make giant figure-8s with your boat (right). Chances are, the fish is still in the vicinity and the action of the baitfish speeding up, turning and slowing down will draw a strike.*

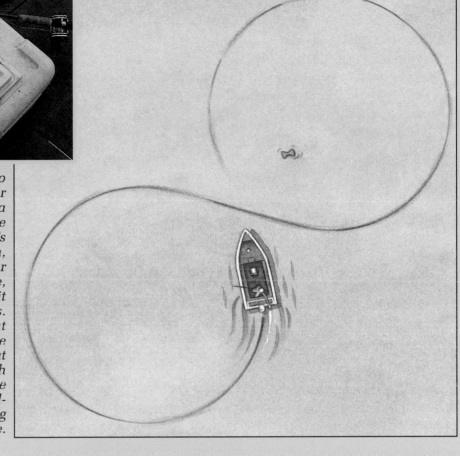

Switchback Technique. *Here's another option for fish that follow but won't strike. Leave the fish alone for 15 minutes or so, then come back and try casting with a different (but similar) lure. But reverse your retrieve angle 180° by positioning your boat on the opposite side of the fish. Sometimes the change of direction triggers a strike. This method is known as the "switchback" technique.*

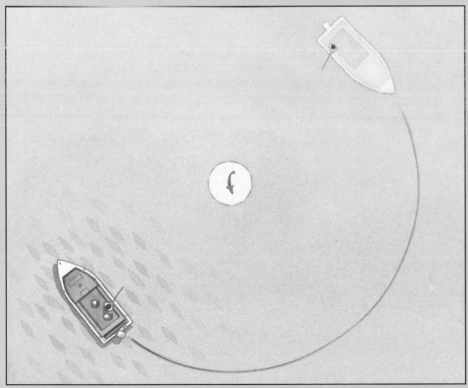

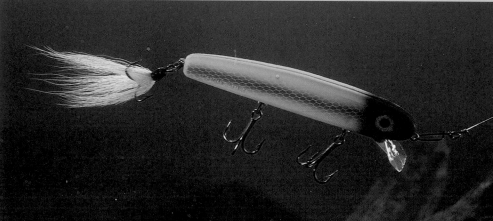

Bucktail Trebles. *Replace the rear treble hook of a crankbait or other subsurface lure with a bucktail-dressed treble. To dress the hook, lay an even layer of bucktail around the hook shank, wrap the ends of the fibers with bright-colored thread and then seal the wraps with epoxy (top). Remove the old hook from the split ring and replace it with the dressed hook to give the lure a billowing action (bottom) that may prompt a half-interested fish to strike.*

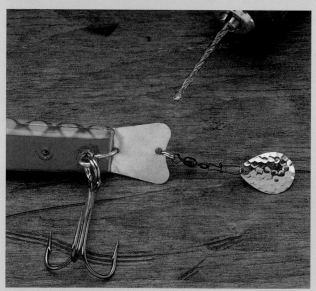

Blade Additions. *Drill a small hole in the center of the metal tail on a jerkbait, then add a split ring, a snap-swivel and a size 1 or 2 spinner blade. Experiment with the color of the blade to determine what the fish prefer on a given day.*

Teaser. *Add a "teaser" to a bucktail by attaching a piece of stainless-steel wire to the rear hook hanger using a haywire twist. Then attach a snap-swivel to the other end of the wire and clip on a small spinner blade.*

REDUCE HANG-UPS

Hang-ups are a constant problem when you're crankin' a rocky reef or point, and nobody wants to lose a $10-plus crankbait.

You could select a shallow runner that will track well above the rocks, but a lure that gets down and bumps them will invariably draw more strikes.

This simple remedy allows you to keep your lure in the strike zone while dramatically cutting down on snags.

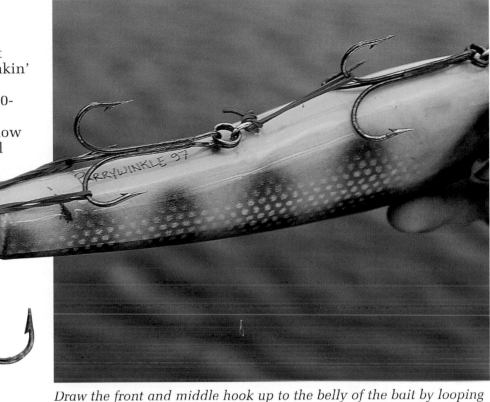

Draw the front and middle hook up to the belly of the bait by looping rubber bands over the hook tines and then securing the rubber bands to the middle and rear hook hangers as shown. This prevents the hooks from dangling beneath the bait where they are more likely to snag.

MID-DEPTH BELIEVER

A Believer is a top pick for muskies and big pike. One reason the bait works so well is that you can fish it shallow or deep, depending on which of the two attachment eyes you use.

Here's a way to modify the lure so it runs at the middle depths, making it even more versatile:

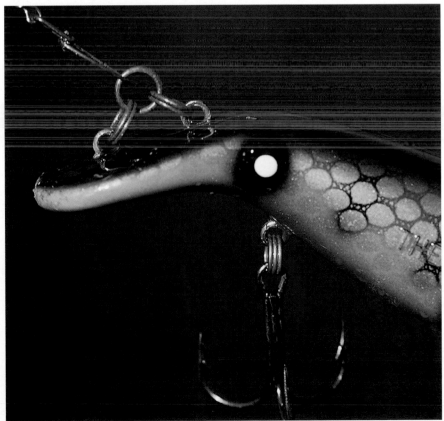

Using a split-ring pliers, attach size 7 split rings to each of the attachment eyes. Then add a third split ring connecting the first two as shown. Clip your leader to the middle ring to make the bait track at an intermediate depth.

WARD OFF WEEDS

Floating weeds are the bane of all pike/muskie trollers. Weeds catch on your line, then slide down to your lure and foul it. And when you're constantly reeling in to clean off your lure, you're not catching fish.

Here's one of those simple solutions that falls into the category "Why didn't I think of that?"

Hold your rod tip just under the surface when trolling in water with lots of floating vegetation. Now the weed sprigs will catch on your rod tip where they can easily be removed, rather than sliding down to your lure.

TETHER YOUR TOOLS

The bottom of every good pike or muskie lake is littered with jaw spreaders, pliers and hook cutters. That's because the fish often go wild when you try to unhook them at boatside, and your tools wind up in the lake.

The solution is to tether to the boat any tools you use for unhooking fish.

Attach each of your tools to a cord and tie the other end of the cord to a cleat on the gunwale. The cord should be at least 8 feet long so it doesn't pull tight when you're try-ing to reach the fish.

UNDERSEAT LURE TUBES

Storing those huge pike and muskie lures is always a problem. Some anglers hang them along the lip of a Styrofoam cooler; that way, they're always handy and the water drains off them so the hooks don't rust.

But a big cooler takes up a lot of space and if a big fish starts thrashing wildly on the boat floor and tips the cooler, you've got a real mess.

Here's a slick way to store your lures so they stay dry and out of the way:

Arrange several pieces of 2-inch PVC tubing around the base of your seat pedestal and rivet them together. Then hang a lure in each tube. If you don't have a rivet gun, you can secure the tubes by wrapping duct tape or wire around the outside of them.

ADD GLIDE TO GLIDERS

The side-to-side action of a glider has a special appeal to pike and muskies. But if you're using a heavy wire leader with a large snap, the lure doesn't have as much lateral movement as it should.

A slight modification will allow the lure to glide farther to the side.

Add a good-sized split ring to the front eye of a glider (inset). This allows the lure to swing more freely and change direction more quickly, adding to its pike/muskie appeal.

SHORE UP SPLIT RINGS

The hooks of many pike and muskie lures are attached with split rings; this way, the hooks are easy to change and they won't bind against the hook hangers.

But when a huge pike or muskie starts thrashing and rolling, the split rings are the first thing to give. Here's how to strengthen your split rings so they'll never open:

1 *Select split rings of two different sizes; the smaller one should fit snugly inside the larger one.*

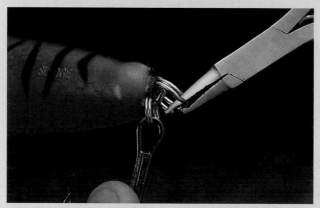

2 *Using a split-ring pliers, connect the hook to the lure with the smaller split ring. Attach the larger ring to the plug and then to the hook.*

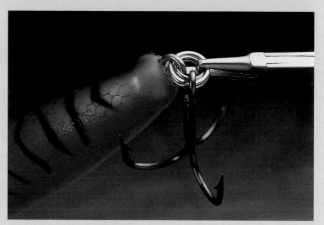

3 *Push the smaller ring into the larger one.*

ROLL 'EM OVER

Not only is it hard to unhook a big muskie or pike thrashing wildly at boatside, it's downright dangerous. If you're not careful, you could wind up with a hook in your hand—and a fish attached to the same lure!

No matter how you unhook your fish, you have to take care to prevent hooking yourself. But here's a way to calm the fish so you can unhook it more easily:

After fighting the fish until it tires, roll it over on its back. In most cases, the fish will relax and stop thrashing long enough for you to remove the hooks. Be sure to use a pair of long-handled pliers to minimize the chances of getting hooked.

Practical Fishing Tips

HOOK-SET SAVVY

One of the biggest problems for the average pike/muskie angler is "getting good hooks," meaning a solid hookset.

When you're fishing a topwater, for example, and you see a fish take your lure, the tendency is to set the hook immediately. But that's usually a mistake; a fish often swirls or slashes at the bait before it actually grabs it. If you set too soon the lure will come flying back at you and the fish will swim away. Always wait until you feel the weight of the fish before setting the hook.

Here are two other tips that will greatly improve your hooking percentage:

Power from the Hips. *Use a long-handled rod and hold it on your hip while retrieving. When a fish grabs your lure, just pivot your hips to get a strong, sideways hookset. If you set with a long, upward sweep of the arms, your wrists and elbows will flex, greatly reducing your power.*

Pull! *When fishing with a jerkbait or other big wooden plug, it's difficult to set the hook because the fish's teeth sink into the wood and you can't get enough leverage to dislodge the lure even if you're using no-stretch line. To increase your hook-setting power, point your rod directly at the fish and pull back in a straight line. This way, you don't lose power through flexing of the rod.*

SAVE YOUR BACK

Lots of pike and muskie anglers develop sore backs from hours of standing up in the boat and pitching heavy lures. That takes all the fun out of your fishing and, if your back is extra-sensitive, will considerably shorten your fishing day.

There are a couple of ways to minimize back soreness:

Heads Up. *Keep your head up and your back straight while retrieving. If you need to look down, just do it with your eyes rather than bending over at the waist and straining your back muscles.*

Back Brace. *Wear an elastic back brace, preferably one with metal stays, to minimize back strain. Some braces are designed to be worn under your clothing; others on the outside of your clothes. Back braces are available through medical supply houses and some sporting goods stores. Wide wader belts used by fly fishermen will also do the job.*

GLO-TAPE FOR NIGHT FISHING

When you're pitching jerk-baits after dark, it's hard to know when to jerk and when to pause because you can't see the lure. And if you're not careful, you'll wind the lure in too far and damage your tip top.

Here's an easy solution:

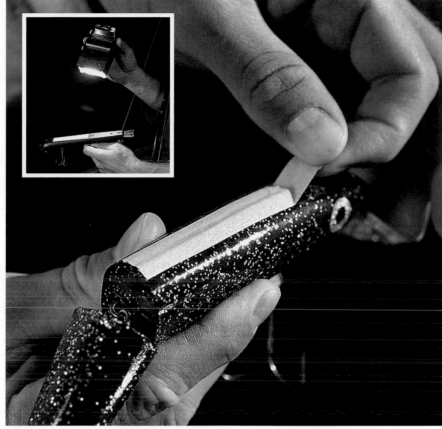

Apply a strip of luminescent (glow-in-the-dark) tape to the back of your jerkbait, then flash it with a camera strobe or bright flashlight (inset). Now you can easily track the lure's movement.

ADD LIFE TO JERKBAITS

Some of the best diver-style jerkbaits are made out of wood, but that can be a problem when you're fishing on a rocky bottom. The nose soon starts to chip and before you know it, the lure doesn't dive the way it should.

Here's how to fix up those expensive jerkbaits so they'll last for years:

Cut a piece of thin metal to fit under the jerkbait's nose; attach the metal with a pair of screws. This way, the metal will take the abuse, saving the wood.

POP-OFF FLOAT FOR BIG BAITS

You need a huge float to support the big minnows used to catch trophy-caliber pike and muskies. The 12- to 15-inch suckers used by some trophy hunters require a cork or Styrofoam float at least 3 and maybe even 4 inches in diameter.

But a float this size has a great deal of resistance, increasing the chances that the fish will drop the bait. So what's an angler to do?

This is how some innovative north country muskie fishermen have solved the problem:

1 *Drill a ³/₈-inch-diameter hole in a 3- to 4-inch cork ball, insert a 3-inch-long dowel the same diameter as the hole and glue it in place. If desired, paint the ball for extra visibility.*

2 *Using a sharp knife, cut a half-inch-long slit in the end of the dowel. Then push your line into the slit.*

3 *When a fish strikes, the line pulls out of the dowel and frees the float. Now the fish can swim off with the bait and feel no resistance.*

Practical Fishing Tips

KEEP BIG BAITS ON THE HOOK

Because pike and muskies almost always swallow their prey headfirst, many anglers like to hook their baitfish in the snout. But when a big, lively baitfish is hooked this way, its struggling often enlarges the hole in its snout and the hook slips out.

Here's some cheap insurance against losing those expensive baitfish:

Cut off an inch-long piece of a heavy rubber band and push one end onto the hook shank. Hook the baitfish through the snout as shown, then push the other end of the rubber band over the hook point and slide it to the top of the snout.

PLAY THE WIND FOR PIKE

It's no secret that pike like cool water. That explains why they're commonly found around spring holes and coldwater inlets during the summer months.

But even if your lake doesn't have an obvious source of cool water, it's important to pay close attention to water temperature differences caused by the wind and then plan your fishing accordingly.

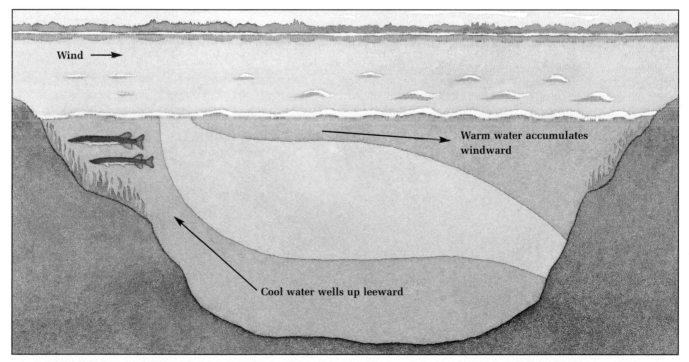

In stratified lakes, an offshore wind pushes the warm surface water away from shore, allowing colder water from the depths to well up and replace it. This means that the water along the lee shore will be considerably cooler than that along the windward shore, sometimes more than 10 degrees cooler.

Pike & Muskie Tips

DOCTORING BUCKTAILS

Bucktail spinners account for more muskies than any other artificial, and they work equally well for big pike.

But not all bucktails are created equal: Some are weighted more heavily than others, some have longer hair that creates a more intense billowing action, and some have blades that produce a stronger beat.

Here's how bucktail specialists doctor their lures to add weight, action and vibration:

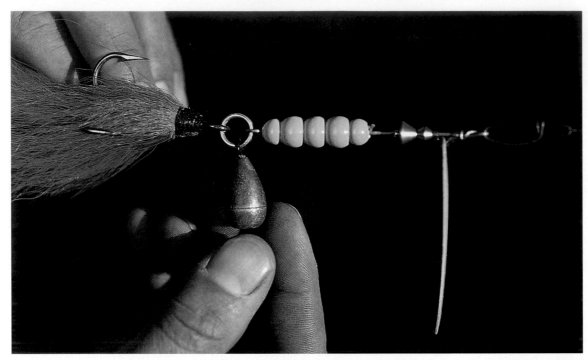

Weight. Clip a Snap-Loc sinker to the ring or eye that holds the treble hook. Carry a selection of sinker sizes so you can weight your bucktails to run at different depths.

Action. Add a split ring and snap to the ring or eye holding the rear treble hook, and then clip on a 2- to 3-inch pork trailer. Don't attach the trailer directly to the treble hook; it will trail too far back, causing short strikes.

Vibration. Drill a hole in the blade of your bucktail, starting on the cupped side.

GO-DEEP SPINNERBAITS

A big-bladed spinnerbait is an excellent choice for drawing muskies and pike out of dense, weedy cover. The large blades produce intense vibrations and create a lot of lift, so you can easily keep the lure above the weedtops.

But there will be times when you want the lure to run deeper in order to fish a deep weedline or deep structure.

Here are three methods for getting spinnerbaits down deep:

Add Lead to Lower Arm. Remove the rubber from a Rubber-Cor sinker and then pinch the slotted lead weight onto the lower arm of the spinnerbait. If you pinch it onto the upper arm, the lure will tip to the side on the retrieve.

Use a Willow-Leaf Blade. *If your spinnerbait has a Colorado blade, remove it and replace it with a willow-leaf blade. A willow-leaf has considerably less lift, so the lure will run deeper.*

Blade/Curlytail Combo. *Remove the top blade of a tandem spinnerbait and replace it with a 4- to 5-inch curlytail grub on a size 6/0 long-shank hook. With only one blade, the lure runs much deeper but still has an appealing action.*

CATFISH TIPS

*C*atfishing isn't always as simple as you think. These refinements will give your success rate a big boost.

LIGHT UP THE NIGHT

Catfish go on the prowl after dark, but landing a big cat at night can be a problem, especially when you're alone. You don't have enough hands to hold your rod, a flashlight and a landing net.

Here's a setup that provides plenty of light and leaves your hands free to fight and land the fish:

Mount 12-volt tractor lights on the bow and stern and aim them into the water. Wire them to a separate marine battery, not your starting battery.

DO-NUTHIN' HOOKSETS

Catfish have a habit of swallowing the hook, which is a big problem if you want to release them. By using a circle hook, which is a special hook first made popular by tuna fishermen, you'll hook most of your fish in the corner of the mouth rather than in the throat.

Circle hooks are also gaining popularity among trotliners and limbliners, because they do not require a strong hookset.

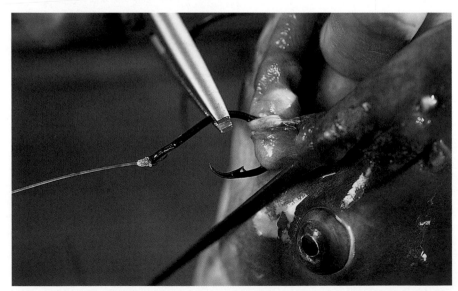

When you get a bite using a circle hook (shown), just wait for the line to tighten as the fish swims off, and then just start reeling. The hook will pivot inside the fish's mouth, almost always lodging in the corner of the jaw.

TWIST-GAFF FOR GIANT CATS

Many catfishermen prefer a gaff to a landing net, but landing a huge cat with an ordinary gaff is a real challenge. Big cats have a habit of twisting as they try to escape, and they can easily twist the gaff right out of your hand.

Here's how to make a gaff that will easily handle the biggest, feistiest cat (or any other big fish):

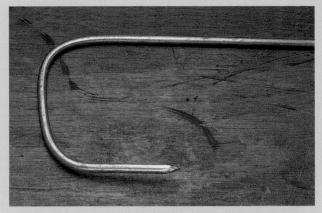

1 *Grind one end of a 36-inch, ¼-inch-diameter steel rod to a sharp point and then bend the end into a hook with a gap of about 4 inches.*

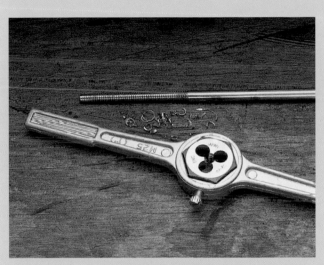

2 *Thread about 2 inches of the other end of the rod, using a threading tool.*

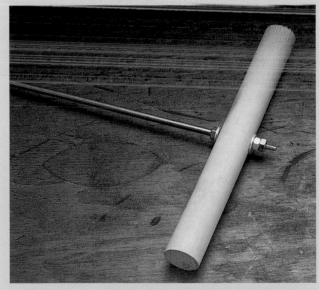

3 *Screw on a nut; add a washer, a wooden handle and another washer; then secure the handle by adding two more nuts. The rod should twist freely inside the handle.*

4 *Gaff a catfish by the jaw. Hold the handle firmly until the fish tires and stops twisting before lifting it into the boat. Because the gaff can spin without the handle turning, you should have no trouble holding on.*

HAND-LAND FLATHEADS

It's hard to imaging sticking your hand into the giant maw of a huge flathead catfish, but that's exactly how many flathead specialists land their fish. And despite the tooth pad on the roof of the fish's mouth (below), they don't even wear gloves. Here's how it's done:

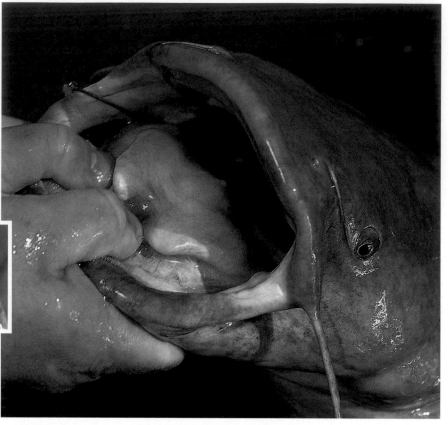

Firmly grab the lower jaw of a flathead as shown (right). Pressing down on the fish's tongue helps prevent the fish from thrashing.

INSIDE-OUT CATALPAS

Catalpa worms, either fresh or frozen, are an excellent catfish bait. But some southern anglers have found a way to make them even more productive. This 3-step process shows you how:

1 *Cut off the head of a catalpa worm using a sharp knife.*

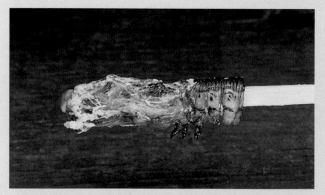

2 *Use a matchstick to push the tail end through the cut end, turning the worm inside out.*

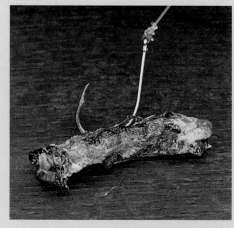

3 *Hook the worm through the body as shown. With the inside of the worm exposed, it emits much more scent.*

COMPACT JUG-FISHING RIG

There's no arguing the effectiveness of jug fishing, but ordinary jug-fishing rigs are bulky, and making them is time consuming.

The rig shown here is compact and easy to build. And you probably already have the makings in your boat.

1 Tie a 2-ounce bell sinker to the end of the cord on an H-shaped marker buoy.

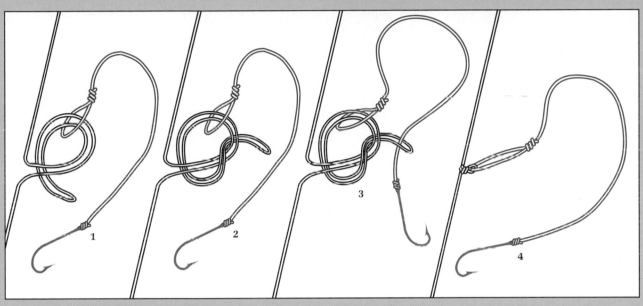

2 Attach droppers at 2- to 3-foot intervals along the cord using dropper loops. To make a dropper loop, (1) double up the cord and pass the loop on the end of the leader over it, (2) tie an overhand knot in the doubled cord, (3) pass the hook through the loop of the doubled cord and (4) pull on the leader to snug up the knot. (Note: These rigs are not recommended for large cats because the fish may hold them under indefinitely).

3 Bait the hooks and then set the depth by making a loop as shown, twisting it twice and then snugging it up on the marker.

4 Toss the buoys upwind of an area you suspect holds cats and then watch them closely as you drift along with them. When a buoy starts to bob erratically, grab it and pull in the fish.

Snag-Proof "Slinky"

When you're fishing cats in heavy cover, you need a snag-resistant sinker. Veteran catmen commonly use a "slinky," which is a piece of hollow nylon cord filled with lead shot. Because of its flexibility, a slinky snakes through rocks, brush or other cover that would surely catch a hard-bodied sinker.

Slinkies are not widely available, but you can easily make your own as shown.

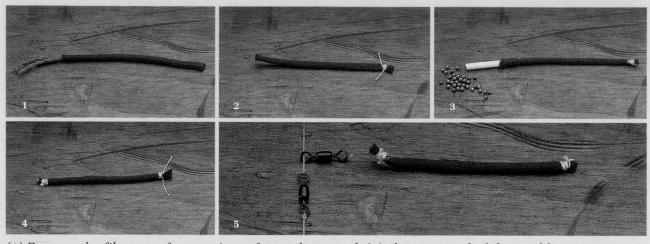

(1) Remove the fiber core from a piece of parachute cord; (2) close one end of the cord by wrapping it with string; (3) insert a drinking straw into the cord, pour in lead shot and remove the straw; (4) wrap the other end of the cord with string and (5) tie a piece of heavy mono to one end of the cord and attach the other end of the mono to a swivel in your line.

Easy Pencil-Lead Rig

A pencil-lead sinker is almost as snag-resistant as a slinky (above). Pencil lead is normally fished on a 3-way surgical-tubing rig (below left), but these rigs are not widely available at tackle shops. Here's how you can make a rig that works even better:

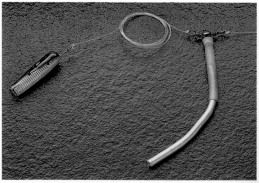

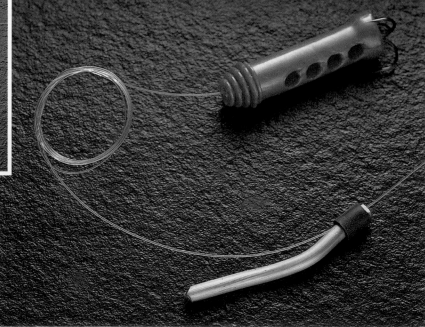

Thread a 1-inch piece of surgical tubing onto your line and then push a piece of pencil lead into the tubing. Pull line through the tubing to adjust your leader length. Should the pencil lead snag, a strong tug will usually pull it out of the tubing and free the rig.

CONVEYOR RIG FOR DENSE-COVER CATS

When cats are buried in heavy timber, even the most snag-proof sinker is of little use. You simply can't get your bait into the dense tangle without getting snagged. But some imaginative catfishermen have come up with a unique way to solve the problem. Here it is:

1 *Stretch a heavy cord from a protruding branch of a submerged tree to another tree branch on shore.*

2 *Attach your line to a sliding clip like the ones used for fishing with trolling boards. Where you attach the clip determines how deep you'll fish.*

3 *Feed line to slide your rig down to the submerged tree. Lock your reel to stop the line in the desired spot.*

4 *When a fish bites, it will pull the line free of the release. The clip will then slide all the way down to the branch. When you want to reset your line, just attach another clip and slide it down to the same spot. When you're done fishing, retrieve all your clips.*

CORMORANTS DRAW CATS

Stands of flooded timber in reservoirs make ideal roosting spots for cormorants. Huge numbers of the birds gather in certain areas and consistently return to the same trees each evening.

Most anglers pay little attention to the birds, but that's a mistake. Here's why:

Cormorant droppings fertilize the water, producing a large crop of plankton which in turn attracts shad. Catfish move in to take advantage of the easy food source.

PREVENT DEEP HOOKING

If you've ever caught a huge catfish and opened its mouth to remove the hook, you know the problem. You can't even see the hook because it's 6 inches down the fish's gullet.

When a fish is hooked that deeply, most anglers just cut the line if they want to release it. But a big hook lodged that deeply in the throat can interfere with a cat's feeding and may eventually kill it.

Here's an easy way to prevent the fish from swallowing the bait:

Tie a bobber stop on your line and then thread the line through a hole in the lid of a film canister before tying on your hook. Slide the bobber stop and canister lid to within a few inches of the hook. Now the fish can take the bait only as deeply as the lid allows.

Practical Fishing Tips

DON'T OVERLOOK OXBOWS

Most rivers change course over time, leaving portions of the old channel separated from the present riverbed. These basins, called oxbows, are connected to the river during high-water periods and often hold surprising numbers of gamefish, including catfish. Fish swim into the oxbows to escape the fast current in the main channel and become trapped when the water recedes.

Here's how you can find oxbows adjacent to your favorite catfish river:

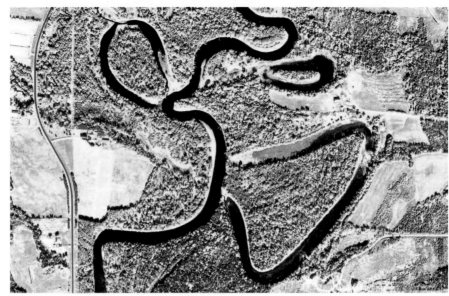

Check an up-to-date map or aerial photo of the river and look for any narrow, half-moon-shaped lakes near the present channel. Oxbows form when high water cuts a new channel across a sharp bend in the river, accounting for the half-moon shape. Try to find an oxbow close to the present river channel so you can carry in a small boat.

SOFT LANDING FOR SOFT BAITS

Soft baits, such as chicken liver, blood bait, paste bait and dip bait, are favorites of many catfish addicts. But they're not such a good choice for long-distance casting. You'll probably snap the bait off the hook when you cast, or the splashdown will rip it off.

Luckily, some innovative catmen have figured out a way to solve the problem:

1 Make a foot-long dropper with a snap on one end and a hook baited with soft bait on the other.

2 Tie a bell sinker to the end of your main line and splice in a large barrel swivel 12 to 18 inches above the sinker.

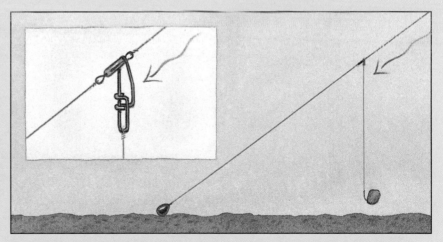

3 Make a long cast, wait for the sinker to hit bottom and tighten up your line. Then snap the dropper onto your line and let it slide down to the barrel swivel. If necessary, pinch a split-shot onto the dropper to help it slide down.

EASY TROTLINE STORAGE

Trotliners commonly set out lines with dozens of hooks. While this "absentee" fishing method is highly effective, the potential for tangles is immense. Most trotliners use a wooden box with enough slots around the edge to hold each dropper.

If you want to try some trotlining but don't have a trotline box to prevent tangles, here's an easy-to-find substitute:

Hang your trotline hooks along the edge of a garbage pail. Any excess line can be neatly piled in the bottom.

ADD FLEX TO LIMBLINES

Another popular absentee fishing method is limblining. You simply dangle a bait from a tree limb hanging over a riverbank and come back and check it the next day. The flexible limb offers little resistance when a cat picks up the bait, and the fish cannot break the line because the springy branch acts as a shock absorber.

But what if there are no springy branches, only stiff ones? Here's how you can add some flex to your limbline:

Cut an inch-wide section out of an inner-tube and then splice it into your limbline as shown.

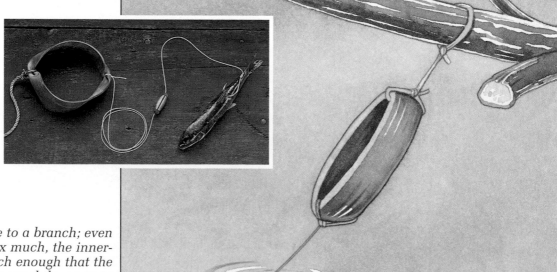

Tie your limbline to a branch; even if it doesn't flex much, the inner-tube will stretch enough that the fish cannot get enough leverage to snap the line.

Night-Light for Jugs

Many jug fishermen set their juglines after dark to take advantage of the nocturnal habits of catfish. But keeping track of the jugs at night is not easy, especially when cats tow them far to the side of the expected drift path.

Some jug fishermen paint their jugs in bright colors to enhance their visibility, but there's a better way:

Wrap a strip of reflective tape around the top of your jugs. Now you can see them from blocks away with a powerful spotlight.

Stop Jugline Tangles

Jug fishermen sometimes set out dozens of jugs to cover a broad expanse of water. As the jugs are retrieved, the lines are usually wrapped around the jugs for storage. But keeping the lines from unwrapping and tangling with other lines is always a problem. Here's an easy solution:

Wrap a large rubber band around the hook bend as shown and then stretch the rubber band around the jug to secure the hook and the line wraps. Keep the rubber band on the jug when the line is in use.

SLOW-RELEASE DIP BAIT

There's no arguing the effectiveness of those stinky concoctions called dip baits but, because of their soupy texture, they start washing away as soon as they hit the water.

Here's how to keep dip baits working a lot longer for you.

1 Smear some dip bait on a piece of sponge and cover it with plastic wrap. Punch a few holes in the wrap.

2 Using a piece of the nylon mesh material used to make spawn bags, gather the corners around the dip bait and tie off the bag.

3 Trim the excess mesh and then push your hook into the bag as shown, leaving the hook point exposed.

BETTER SCENT DISPENSER

Rather than dipping their baits in scent, savvy catfishermen dip a piece of foam rubber in the scent and slide the foam onto the hook. This way, the scent doesn't wash off as quickly.

But ordinary foam rubber is quite porous, so the scent still washes away in a few minutes. Chances are you have a better scent dispenser in your medicine chest or gun cabinet:

Push a foam-rubber earplug onto the shank of your hook and then let it soak in scent for a few minutes. The density of an earplug is much greater than that of ordinary foam rubber, so the scent won't wash out as fast. The earplug is also quite buoyant, so it will float your bait off the bottom.

ADD WOBBLE TO SHAD

Shad are an important catfish food in many rivers and reservoirs, and they're a favorite bait of many catfishermen. But shad are one of the least hardy baitfish, so most anglers fish them dead or use them as cut bait, relying on their strong scent to draw cats.

If you're fishing in moving water, you can add visual appeal to shad, further increasing their effectiveness. Here's how:

Thread a small shad onto a size 3/0 to 5/0 Kahle (wide-bend) hook as shown, leaving the hook point inside the fish. With the tail curled around the hook, the shad will flutter enticingly in the current.

TRIMMING TAIL DRAWS CATS

Everyone knows that cats are scent-oriented, but they rely on their vision and lateral-line sense as well. Here's a simple way of doctoring a baitfish so it appeals to *all* of a catfish's important senses:

Trim the tail of a baitfish using a pair of scissors. This increases the flow of body fluids into the water for more scent, and the clipped tail makes the baitfish swim harder to maintain its balance, enhancing its visual appeal and producing more vibrations.

3-Way Slip-Rig

Big cats have a way of burying themselves among logs, rocks or other heavy cover that almost ensures that you'll snag up if you use an ordinary slip-sinker rig. You could use a 3-way rig to keep your hook above the cover, but an ordinary 3-way doesn't slip, so some cats will feel resistance and drop the bait.

The solution is to use a hybrid rig that combines the qualities of both a 3-way and a slip-sinker rig.

Make a dropper of the desired length with a bell sinker on one end and a barrel swivel on the other. Thread the barrel swivel onto your line, then tie another barrel swivel to the end of your line and add your leader. The dropper and leader should be slightly lighter than your main line; that way, you won't lose the whole rig if you get snagged.

Emergency Slip-Sinker

Frequent hang-ups are a fact of life when you're fishing in snaggy cover. If you're using a fixed-sinker rig and run out of weights, you can substitute an old bolt, a piece of pipe or most any other kind of "junkyard" sinker. But if you're using a slip-sinker rig, a substitute weight is not as easy to find.

At left is an emergency slip-sinker that you can probably find in your tool box.

Make a slip-sinker from an old spark plug by bending the electrode over your line as shown. Add a bead to cushion your knot and prevent your swivel from slipping through the gap in the electrode.

TAME WILD CATS

When you catch a big catfish that you want to release, it's best to keep the fish in the water and unhook it at boatside. That way, it won't get injured while flopping around in the boat, and the boat floor won't get covered with slime and blood.

But unhooking a powerful cat while it's thrashing at boatside is easier said than done. Here's how to make the job go a lot smoother:

Have your partner hold the fish's tail while you remove the hook. With its tail immobilized, the fish will stop struggling long enough for you to unhook it.

FLATHEAD FAVORITES

Flatheads have a penchant for live baitfish, especially those that are a part of their normal diet. This explains the effectiveness of two of the most common fish that swim in North American waters: bullheads and sunfish.

You probably won't find these fish at your local bait shop, so you'll have to catch your own. But if you live near a shallow, fertile warmwater lake or stream, that shouldn't be a problem. Be sure to check your state's regulations, however, before using these species for bait.

Here's how to hook bullheads and sunfish:

Bullheads. *Hook a 5- to 12-inch bullhead just ahead of the adipose fin.*

Sunfish. *Hook a 4- to 7-inch sunfish through the back below the rear base of the dorsal fin.*

TROUT & SALMON TIPS

The selective feeding habits of these coldwater dwellers explain why anglers have devised so many clever schemes for enticing them to strike.

A BETTER SPLIT-SHOT RIG

Stream-trout anglers rely heavily on split-shot rigs for presenting natural bait naturally. When weighted with a split-shot of the proper size, the bait drifts at exactly the same speed as the current so it looks like real food.

But split-shot have some drawbacks: Because they're pinched onto the line, they don't slip when a fish takes the bait. And they tend to wedge in the rocks, so the rig won't drift at all.

Here's a split-shot substitute that will solve both of these problems:

Thread a leader sleeve onto your line and add a bobber stop to keep it in the desired position. The sleeve acts as a mini slip-sinker, allowing trout to take the bait without feeling resistance. And its thin shape reduces the chances of snagging. Carry a selection of different-sized sleeves for different depths and current speeds (right).

CONTROL YOUR DRIFT

Casting to stream trout while drifting with the current not only enables you to cover a lot of water, it minimizes "drag" (the telltale wake left by a lure or bait that is not drifting naturally).

Ideally, your boat will drift straight downstream in the same position so you can establish a consistent casting pattern. But when you're fishing in the wind, that's usually not the case; the boat will swing from side-to-side and sometimes turn end-for-end.

You could try to control your drift with a trolling motor, but there's an easier way:

Attach a heavy chain to a rope, tie the rope to your bow eye and drop the chain to the bottom before starting your drift. The chain keeps your bow pointing straight upstream as you drift (top). The rope should be long enough to easily reach bottom, but not long enough to reach your outboard. This way, you can motor back upstream without lifting the chain (bottom).

EASY-TO-TIE SNELL

If you're a serious trout or salmon angler, it's a good idea to learn how to tie a snell. The knot comes in handy not only for attaching hooks, but also for making yarn flies and loops for holding fresh spawn.

There are several ways to tie a snell, but the method shown here is undoubtedly the easiest and fastest:

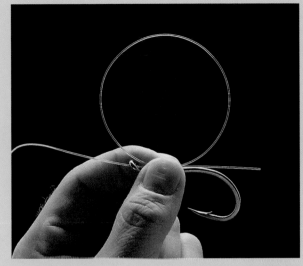

1 Push your line through the eye of a bait hook (preferably one with an upturned eye) and make a 3-inch loop over the back of the hook as shown. The tag end should extend just past the hook bend.

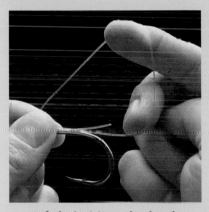

2 While holding the hook and loop with your left hand, insert the first two fingers of your right hand into the loop.

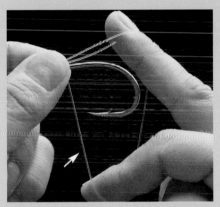

3 Twist your fingers to begin wrapping the front leg of the loop (arrow) around the hook, the back leg of the loop and the standing line.

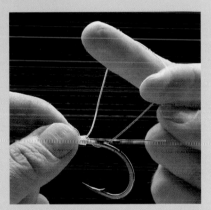

4 Twist your fingers again to continue wrapping the front leg around the hook, the back leg and the standing line. Continue twisting and wrapping this way at least six times.

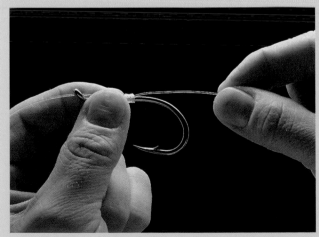

5 While holding the wraps with the fingers of your left hand, pull on the standing line and tag end with your right hand to snug up the snell.

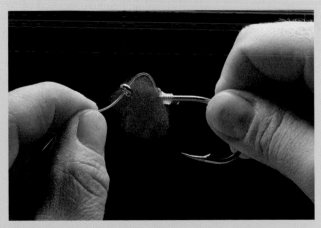

6 To make a yarn fly, insert a piece of yarn under the line between the snell and the hook eye, then pull on the standing line to slide the snell up to the eye and secure the yarn.

TWO-WAY STEELHEAD RIG

Big-river steelhead trollers often use crankbaits to pull bait rigs down into deep runs and give them extra action. To prevent fouling, the crankbait's hooks are removed and the bait rig is attached to the lure's front hook hanger.

But steelhead sometimes strike the hookless crankbait rather than the bait rig. Here's how you can catch those fish without the bait rig constantly tangling in the crankbait's hooks:

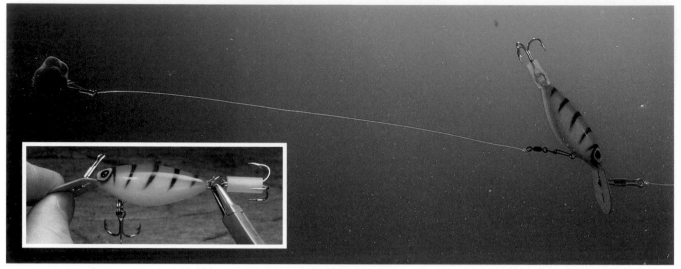

Slide a piece of surgical tubing onto the shank of a treble hook you removed. Attach the hook to the rear hook hanger with a split ring and then push the surgical tubing over the split ring and rear hook hanger (inset) to make the hook stand out straight. This way, it will not foul the trailing bait rig but will hook most steelhead that strike the plug.

GET DOWN WITH LIGHT SPINNERS

Unweighted in-line spinners with big, fluorescent-colored blades are a favorite of salmon anglers. But these lightweight lures don't cast well and it's difficult to get them down to fish deep runs because the big blades have so much lift.

If your spinner has plastic beads or other plastic spacers, as most lures of this type do, there's an easy way to solve the problem:

Using a pair of pliers, crack a couple of the center beads to remove them from the shaft. Then pinch on split-shot to replace them. Be advised, however, that lead-weighted lures are not allowed in some salmon streams; check your regulations.

IN-LINE SWIVEL

Thin trolling spoons are popular among trout and salmon anglers because they have plenty of wobble at slow speed. In order to change spoons easily, most fishermen attach them with a snap-swivel.

The problem is, the weight of a good-sized snap-swivel will reduce the wobble of these nearly weightless spoons. Here's how to rig trolling spoons so they have better action and catch more fish:

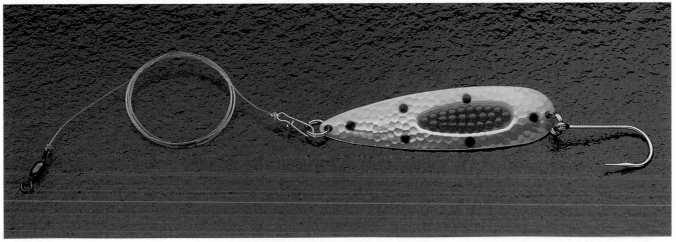

Splice a barrel or bead-chain swivel into your line about 2 feet from the end, then add a Cross-Loc snap. You'll still be able to change spoons easily but the snap, by itself, won't affect the spoon's action.

MINI-TEASER FOR STREAMERS

Most streamers are tied with flashy or bright-colored materials to catch the eye of good-sized trout or salmon. But discolored water greatly reduces the visual appeal of these flies.

Here's how you can improve a streamer's visual appeal while adding vibration that will attract fish even in muddy water:

Push a small barrel swivel over the hook point (flatten the barb if necessary), attach a split ring to the other eye of the swivel, then add a size 00 spinner blade to the split ring. Secure the swivel on the hook with a tab punched from a plastic lid. Be sure the fly's wing is short enough that it doesn't inhibit rotation of the spinner blade.

HARNESS YOUR HOOKSETS

Novice fly fishermen often make the mistake of setting the hook by snapping their wrist and rearing back with their arm, as a bass angler might do. But with a soft-tipped fly rod, all you accomplish with that type of hook-set is putting a big bend in the rod. To make matters worse, your line flies out of the water, spooking any fish in the area.

Here's how to get a stronger hookset with a lot less effort:

Set the hook by lifting the rod horizontally with a stiff wrist while rapidly stripping line (arrow) with the other hand. You'll be surprised at how much hook-setting power you can generate. And when you make your next cast, the other fish will still be out there.

ROLL AWAY SNAGS

If you're fly fishing in water with a lot of woody cover, snags are a constant problem, especially when you're using a light tippet. Most fishermen just snap off the fly and tie on a new one.

But if you know how to make a roll cast, you might be able to save your fly. Here's the trick:

When your fly snags, raise your rod tip and then throw a loop as you would when making a roll cast. The force created by the loop unrolling on the opposite side of the snag often frees your fly.

NIGHT-FISHING TIPS

It's easy to understand why so many accomplished fly fishermen are night stalkers. Not only do many heavy insect hatches occur after dark, you can move about more freely without the trout detecting you.

But night fishing can also be very frustrating. Your line and fly are difficult to see, so your casting accuracy suffers and you'll miss more fish because you don't set the hook when you should. And if you want to change flies, tying on a new one is a real challenge.

Here are some suggestions that will make your night fishing more enjoyable—and more productive:

Visible Fly. *Tie on a fly that has some light-colored dressing on the front end. This way the fly is highly visible to you, yet not so bright that it looks unnatural to the fish.*

Tiny Clip. *Instead of tying on your fly, attach it with a tiny clip such as a Fas-Snap. This way you can easily remove your old fly and snap on a new one.*

Bright Line. *Spool up with light-colored (preferably white) fly line. Even if you can't see your fly, the light-colored line will help you pinpoint its location.*

JIG SHALLOW FOR DEEPWATER LAKERS

When you're vertically jigging for deepwater lakers, your graph will often display a layer of fish scattered over a depth range of 10 feet or more.

The tendency is to drop your lure right into the fish zone and jig it right in the face of the trout. But that's usually not a good idea. Here's a better strategy:

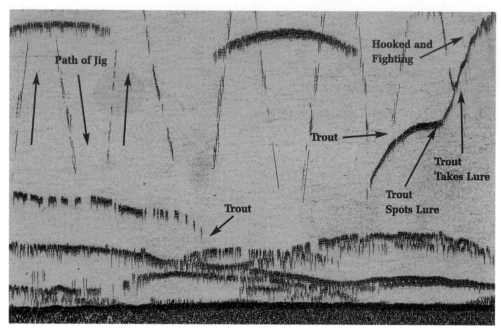

Watch your graph closely and jig a few feet above the highest fish. If you hold your boat stationary, you should be able to see your lure and the fish at the same time. Lakers are accustomed to looking up for their food, and they're more likely to go after a bait fished above them than one at their own depth. You may even be able to see the path of your lure and lakers coming up to take it.

"CUSHION" FOR SUPERLINE

Lots of anglers troll with 3-way rigs to reach lakers in deep water. They spool their reels with superline which gets down much faster than mono because of its thin diameter. And the low stretch factor of superline means stronger hooksets.

But there's a major downside to using superline in this situation: The jagged rocks that typically pave the bottom in laker habitat can sheer off superline in a heartbeat, so you lose your entire rig.

Rather than constantly retying your rig, try this:

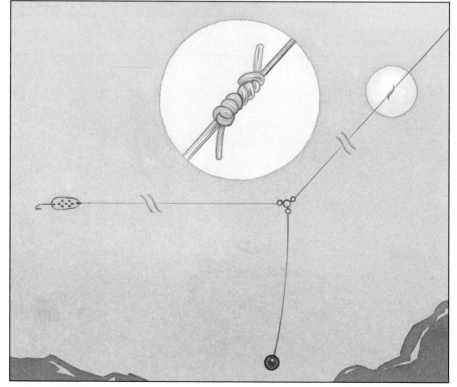

Splice about 4 feet of 25- to 30-pound-test mono onto the end of your superline using a double uni-knot (p. 27). The mono "cushion" will withstand much more abrasion than the plain superline, so you'll rarely break off in the rocks.

DEEPWATER MARKER

Lake trout commonly hold in tight schools at depths of 60 to 100 feet or even more. When you find one of these schools, it's a good idea to precisely mark the spot. The problem is, an ordinary dumbbell-style marker may not have enough string to reach the bottom and, even if it does, it will take you forever to wrap that much string around the narrow spool.

Instead of wasting your fishing time wrapping string, try this:

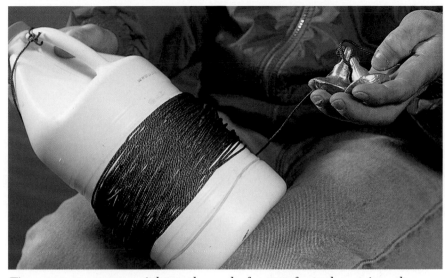

Tie a 6- to 8-ounce weight to the end of a 100-foot-plus string, then attach the string to the handle of a 1-gallon bleach jug. To secure the marker for storage, wrap the string around the body of the jug and stretch a heavy rubber band over the string and weight.

PRECISION JIGGING

When you're vertical jigging for trout in those tight schools, your boat control must be near perfect. If you let the wind push you even a little off the spot, you won't catch a thing.

You could use a trolling motor to stay on top of the fish, but there's an easier way:

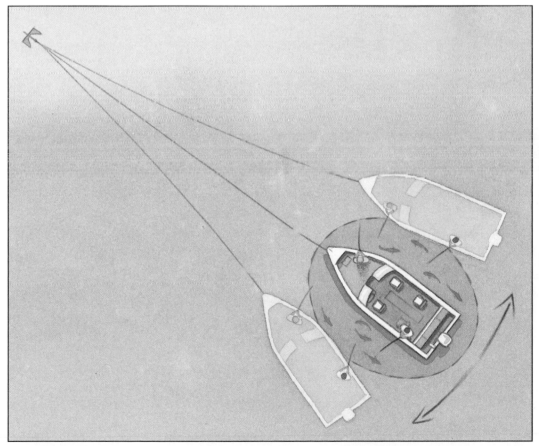

Drop a heavy anchor (25 to 30 pounds) straight upwind of the trout school, let out enough anchor rope so your boat drifts directly over the trout school and then tie the rope to your bow eye. Depending on the strength of the wind, your anchor rope should be 2 to 3 times as long as the water is deep. Now you can jig vertically as your boat swings back and forth over the fish.

THINK BIG FOR GIANT LAKERS

It's not unusual for a huge lake trout to eat a whitefish or other fish that measures half of its own length. This means that a 40-pound laker can eat a fish up to 2 feet long. Yet most anglers try to catch these monster trout using baits no more than 6 inches long, usually with little success.

If those giant lakers are eluding you, try thinking big:

1 Push a size 8/0 single hook into the nose and out the side of a 10-inch tubebait. Make an 8-inch-long trailer using a piece of 20-pound-test mono with a size 4/0 treble hook on one end and a large snap-swivel on the other. Then clip the snap to the bend of the single hook.

2 Attach the single hook to the "pigtail" on the rear of a 10- to 14-inch dodger or flasher, such as the Luhr Jensen Abe 'n' Al. If desired, add a strip of belly meat to the treble hook for a little extra scent.

3 Troll the rig, which can be up to 2 feet in length, on a 3-way swivel rig with a 10-ounce weight or on a downrigger. The flasher gives the bait a wide swimming action that has a special appeal to trophy-class lakers.

PAY ATTENTION TO PLUMES

River mouths are key locations for big-lake salmon and trout. Fish that were hatched in a particular river (or stocked there) home back to the same river at spawning time, and knowledgeable anglers know right when to be there.

But river mouths attract salmon and trout at other times of the year as well. Where a plume of warm water flows into a coldwater lake, for example, you'll often find a mixing zone where the water temperature is just right for the fish.

Here's how to find salmon and trout that are relating to plumes of river water:

Look for color changes that reveal the location of plumes of river water. In a clear lake, the plumes may be brownish or greenish and the surrounding water bluish. Often the wind or current pushes the plume away from the river mouth. If the wind is from the north, for example, the plume will spread to the south, and so will the fish.

REVIVE "GASSY" TROUT

In lake trout and other salmonids, the swim bladder is connected to the esophagus, enabling the fish to "burp" up gas that builds up from the water pressure change when you reel them up from deep water. This explains the trail of bubbles you see when you're fighting the fish.

But you'll occasionally hook a laker that for some reason can't burp up the gas. It becomes bloated and unable to swim back down when released. It will wallow around on the surface for awhile and eventually die.

If you had an extra-long hypodermic needle, you could try "fizzing" the fish to let out the gas. If you're fishing with downriggers, however, there's a better solution:

Tie a small hook to a piece of 6-pound mono and attach the line to your downrigger ball. Imbed the hook in the trout's chin and then slowly lower the ball to pull the trout back down, increasing the water pressure and compressing the gas. When you feel the ball hit the bottom, crank it up rapidly; the light line will break and the trout (or any other deep-caught fish) will swim away with only a small hook as a souvenir of its ordeal.

SPICE UP SPOONS

Big spoons, such as the Eppinger Husky Devle, account for impressive numbers of trophy-caliber lake trout. Not only do these lures attract fish because of their color and flash, they move enough water that lakers can easily track them using their lateral-line sense.

But lakers are extremely scent-oriented, so these spoons are even more effective when they leave a scent trail. Here's how to rig them so they do just that:

1 Make a 5-inch trailer-hook setup from a piece of 20-pound mono: Tie a size 4/0 treble hook to one end and a large barrel swivel to the other. Attach the barrel swivel to the lure's rear split ring.

2 Cut a strip of meat (skin attached) about 6 inches long, 1 inch wide and ¼ inch thick from a whitefish, cisco or other oily baitfish. Or, where legal, use belly meat from a lake trout you've cleaned. Then cut the strip diagonally (inset) to make 2 tapered pieces.

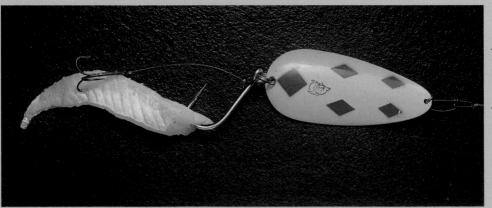

3 Push the spoon's hook through the front end of the meat strip and the trailer hook through the back end. Then let out a few feet of line and troll the lure at normal speed. It should wobble widely; if it doesn't, trim the strip until it no longer restricts the spoon's action.

Practical Fishing Tips

LET IT SLIDE

The Luhr Jensen J-Plug is a time-proven salmon lure. When trolled at high speed (3 to 4 mph), it has an erratic darting action that will often draw strikes when lures with a more predictable action won't.

But if you clip a J-Plug to your line like most fishermen do, you're taking away one of the lure's most important attributes. Here's the right way to attach a J-Plug:

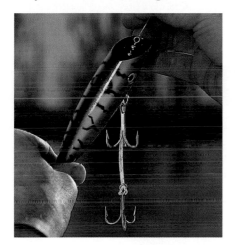

Push the bead-chain through the hole at the front of the lure and tie your line directly to the attachment eye (left). This way, the lure can slide up your line when you're fighting a fish. A clip or snap-swivel would prevent the lure from sliding up, so a fish can use the lure to get more leverage to shake the hook.

J-PLUG STORAGE

Serious salmon anglers may carry dozens of J-Plugs in assorted colors and sizes. To avoid tangling, the plug bodies and hook harnesses must be stored separately.

If you put several of the conical bodies in a tackle box tray, however, they'll rub against each other and ruin the finish.

Here's a good way to store your J-Plugs so they'll last for years:

Remove the trays from a tackle box and cut a piece of plastic or plywood to fit in the box as shown. Drill several rows of holes of the size needed for your plug bodies and then glue the plastic or plywood in place. Set the plugs in the holes (head up) and keep the hooks in a small utility box.

Jettison Heavy Weights

Anglers trolling for lake trout and salmon often use weights as heavy as 1 pound to get their lures into the 60- to 100-foot depth range that the fish commonly inhabit.

But that much weight on the line not only dampens the fight, it increases the chances of losing the fish.

Here's how to rig your weights so that won't happen:

1 Tie a piece of 20-pound-test mono to a heavy weight and make a loop in the other end of the line. Then thread a jettison release onto your fishing line.

2 Position the release as far up the line as you want it, put the loop into the slot and then push the peg into the hole to secure the release on the line.

3 The force of a strike pulls the pin out of the hole, releasing the weight. Now you can fight the fish on a free line. When you're ready to reset your line, just add a new weight.

Stopping "Screamers"

When you hook a big salmon or trout, it often makes a spectacular initial run. Unless you have a reel that holds a lot of line, you might get spooled.

If you've tied into a "screamer" and your spool is starting to show, here's a trick that could save the day:

Instead of putting more pressure on the fish in an attempt to slow it down, release the pressure altogether by pushing your free spool button and then lightly thumbing the reel to prevent an overrun. When the fish no longer feels resistance, it will usually stop running. Then you can close the distance with your boat to get some line back.

    Practical Fishing Tips

Add "Kick" to Your Fly

A dodger-fly combo is an excellent choice for finicky trout and salmon. The dodger produces enough flash to attract fish from a distance, and its intense wobble gives the fly some action.

Most trolling flies come pre-rigged with a 24- to 30-inch leader which is then attached to the pigtail at the rear of the dodger.

But with a leader that long, the fly may not have enough action to trigger strikes. Here's how to give your fly extra fish appeal:

Shorten your leader so it's 1.5 to 2 times the length of your dodger. For example: If you're using a size 0 dodger, which is about 8 inches long, your leader should be 12 to 16 inches long. This way the wobble of the dodger will give the fly a sharper kick.

Quick Color Change

No other gamefish are as color conscious as salmon. On a given day, they'll repeatedly strike a silver spoon with a green stripe but ignore a similar spoon with a blue stripe. But on the next day, they may want the blue-striped spoon.

You could spend a small fortune investing in lures of every possible color, but here's a better solution:

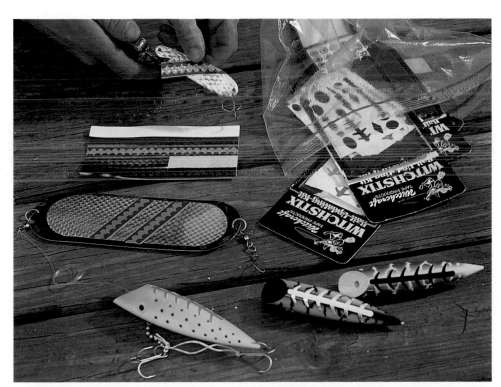

Carry a good supply of lure tape in a variety of colors. Place a diagonal strip of tape across the convex side of your spoon and then trim the edges with a sharp knife. You can also use the tape to add a little color to plugs and even dodgers.

ICE-FISHING TIPS

*T*here's a lot more to ice fishing than sitting on a stool, staring down an ice hole and waiting for the fish to bite.

ICE FISHING: A DETAIL GAME

If you've ever been sitting next to another ice fisherman, watching him haul in fish after fish while you're not getting a nibble, you know how much the little things matter in ice fishing.

Gamefish in near-freezing water are much less aggressive than those in warm water, so you have to do everything just right to convince them to bite. That means finding exactly the right spot, using the right gear and finding the presentation that the fish want on a given day—which may be a lot different than the one they wanted a day earlier.

Even when you're doing everything right, ice fishing can be a real pain because your bait freezes up, your hole won't stay open, your rod guides freeze shut, your reel gets caked with ice, and any of a hundred other challenges. But there are remedies for these common problems that will make your ice-fishing adventure a lot more enjoyable.

DON'T FOLLOW THE CROWD

When you see a lot of ice fishermen working the same area, there's a real temptation to join the crowd. But that's usually a mistake; your chances are better if you find your own spot where the fish haven't been hassled.

Savvy ice fishermen use handheld GPS units to pinpoint spots they fish in summer and then drive a snowmobile or 4-wheeler to these locations, which are often far from the main road.

But the batteries in handheld units don't last long in winter, and it's difficult to see the small screens when you're speeding out to your spot. Here's the solution:

Attach a mounting bracket for your GPS to the dash of your snowmobile or 4-wheeler and wire the unit to your starting battery. This way, you can easily see the screen while driving and you won't have to worry about your battery going dead. Before leaving shore, be sure to punch in the position in case a storm blows up later in the day.

UNDERWATER EYES

An underwater video camera gives you a big edge in ice fishing because it not only tells you what kind of fish are down there, it shows you exactly what you have to do to make them bite. Here's the basic strategy:

1 Drill a hole for the camera a couple of feet away from your fishing hole and then twist the cord until the camera is pointing right at your lure.

2 Watch how the fish react to different presentations. If you're jigging, for example, and a sharp snap of the rod sends the fish darting away, try a much more subtle movement. On some days, you'll find that the fish don't want any movement at all.

A LITTLE SQUIRT

If you pour a little water on clear ice, you can sound right through the ice to determine the right depth *before* drilling your holes. That saves a lot of time and energy, but where do you find the water to get started?

You could pour some water out of your minnow bucket, but there's a better way. Carry some water in a spray bottle and squirt a little on the ice where you want to sound. Adding a little salt to the water will help keep the bottle from freezing up. Don't fill your squirt bottle with antifreeze or alcohol; using them for this purpose is bad for the environment and illegal almost everywhere.

LATE-SEASON SOUNDING

Sounding through the ice is easy in early season, when the ice is usually clear. But after a heavy snowfall and some freezing and thawing, the ice turns milky and may have a lot of air bubbles frozen into it. At that point, you probably won't be able to get a good depth reading.

You could drill some holes to take your soundings, but that means a lot of extra work because some of the holes will be at the wrong depth. Here's how to make those late-season soundings without drilling:

Look for old fishing holes that have recently frozen; the ice there will be clear. Just squirt a little water on the ice and take your sounding as you would in early season.

TAPER YOUR HOLE

When you're fighting a pike, lake trout or other big, powerful fish, it's difficult to get its head started up the hole. Some anglers carry a gaff to hook the fish when it gets close, but that's not a good idea if you're into catch and release.

To improve your odds of landing the fish and avoiding injury to it, taper the bottom of the hole (right) so you can get the fish started more easily. Here are two ways to do the job:

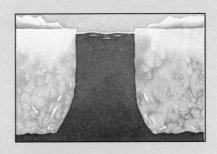

Chisel It. *After drilling your hole, use an ice chisel to taper the bottom. Just walk around the hole while chopping at a 45° angle as shown.*

Auger It. *Use an auger with a blade designed to flare the bottom of the hole. You'll get a much smoother taper than you could with a chisel.*

ILLUMINATE YOUR HOLES

After dark, it's hard to see your float. Even if you set a lantern on the ice, the float will probably be in shadow. Instead of setting your lantern on the ice, set it *in* the ice. This way, the hole will be backlit and your float will be much easier to see.

Drill a pair of holes in the ice a few feet apart and then drill a third hole in the middle for your lantern. The hole for the lantern should almost, but not quite, break through the ice (left). Now the lantern's glow will penetrate through the ice, lighting your holes from below and greatly improving your visibility.

NO MORE FROZEN REELS

A small spinning reel is ideal for many kinds of ice fishing, but there's one problem: Snow and slush collect on the spool and bail, and will freeze if you set the reel on the ice (inset), so you'll have to chip it off with your fingers. Here's a good solution:

Substitute an "underspin," which is a closed-face, trigger-operated spinning reel, for your open-face reel. The spool is covered and there is no bail, so snow or slush buildup is not a problem.

FREEZE-PROOF FLOAT

Lots of ice fishermen rely on small floats to detect light bites, but ordinary floats soon become caked with ice, which is hard to remove. A simple piece of equipment eliminates the freeze-up headache:

Substitute a sponge float for an ordinary hard-bodied float. When ice starts to build up, just squeeze the float with your fingers and the ice will crumble away.

INSULATE YOUR FISH

Most anglers just toss the fish they catch on the ice and let them freeze solid. But what do you do with the fish when you get home? They're too stiff to clean, so you have to set them in the sink and let them thaw out, which may not go over too well with the rest of the family. Luckily, there's an easy solution:

Put a layer of snow in a 5-gallon bucket, throw in some fish and then cover them with another layer of snow. Snow is an excellent insulator and will prevent the fish from freezing solid, even at below-zero temperatures.

Minnow Mobility

It's no secret that mobility is the key to ice-fishing success, but how can you be mobile when you have to lug around bulky gear, like a minnow bucket? Here's how anglers who tip their jigs with minnow heads solve the problem:

Put some minnows into a small, resealable plastic bag and carry it in your shirt pocket. When you're using only the heads for tipping, the minnows do not have to be alive and your body heat will prevent them from freezing.

Permanent Minnow Supply

It's hard to keep leftover minnows in winter. If you set them outside, your bucket will freeze solid; if you bring them inside, you'll soon have a stinky mess.

But anglers who fish in a permanent shack can easily keep their minnows alive for weeks. Here's how:

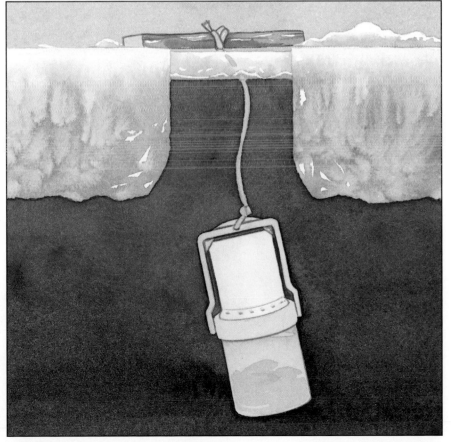

Put your leftover minnows in a small "leech" bucket or other flow-thru bucket small enough to fit into an ice hole. Tie a string to the handle, lower the bucket beneath the level of the ice and then tie a stick onto the string and set it on the ice. On your next outing, use a chisel to open the hole and remove the bucket.

FINE-TUNING YOUR TIP-UP

Spindle-type tip-ups are popular among anglers fishing for pike, walleyes, lake trout and other large gamefish. These tip-ups have an underwater reel that won't freeze up and are sensitive enough to signal a very light bite. But they can be accidentally tripped by an overactive minnow or a nibbling panfish.

Most anglers don't realize that it's possible to adjust the tension setting to suit the type of fishing they're doing. By changing the position of the flag in relation to the spindle, you can achieve the following 4 tension settings:

Very Light. *Position the flag arm under the smooth end of the spindle with the spindle turning away from the flag (arrow).*

Light. *Position the flag arm under the smooth end of the spindle with the spindle turning toward the flag (arrow).*

Medium. *Position the flag arm under the notched end of the spindle with the spindle turning away from the flag (arrow).*

Heavy. *Position the flag arm under the notched end of the spindle with the spindle turning toward the flag (arrow).*

NO-FREEZE WIND TIP-UP

There are times when a wind tip-up will catch more fish than an ordinary tip-up, because the wind blowing on the arm plate keeps your bait moving. But unlike a spindle tip-up (opposite), a wind tip-up has an exposed reel, so your line may freeze into the ice in cold weather.

Here's how to keep your line moving freely, even when your hole is freezing up:

Push a piece of ¾-inch plastic tube through a block of Styrofoam, then feed your line through the tube and set the block into the hole. Pour a little vegetable oil into the tube to prevent ice from forming. Now your line can move freely in even the coldest weather.

TIP-UP DEPTH MARKER

When you set your tip-up, you probably use a snap-on depth finder (below) to determine the right depth. But when a fish trips your flag, you'll lose that setting. Here's how to avoid having to reset your depth every time you catch a fish.

Once you determine the right depth, pinch a small split-shot onto your line just below the tip-up spool. The shot won't prevent the fish from taking line and, when you want to reset your depth, just reel the shot back to the same position.

EMERGENCY TIP-UP

If you get to the lake and discover that you forgot your tip-ups at home, don't panic. If there are some willows growing along shoreline, you have a ready-made substitute. In fact, some veteran anglers prefer willow tip-ups to the real thing because the resistance offered by the flexing branch makes the fish take the bait harder than normal.

1 Cut some live willow sticks along the lakeshore and remove any small branchlets. Push a 24- to 36-inch willow stick into a pile of slush removed from your hole. The end of the willow should be directly above the middle of the hole.

2 Add a hook and split-shot to the end of a small spool of line and then lay the spool in a depression in the snow alongside your hole.

3 Lower the rig to the desired depth, tie a loop in the line and then drape the loop over the end of the willow.

4 Watch the willow carefully; a sharp bend signals a bite. The willow offers only light resistance, so the fish is not likely to drop the bait.

5 When a fish makes a strong run, it will pull the loop off the willow and the spool will spin freely as the fish takes line. Set the hook when the fish stops running.

ADD LIFE TO HANDWARMERS

Those chemical handwarmers are lifesavers in frigid weather. Once you open the packets, the chemical reaction begins and lasts for 8 to 12 hours, enough to get you through a long day of fishing. But what if you don't want to fish all day?

Here's how you can stop the chemical reaction and save those expensive handwarmers for another day:

Place the handwarmer packets in a small resealable plastic bag. The chemical reaction requires oxygen, and when the packets use up the oxygen in the bag, the reaction stops. When you take the packets out of the bag, they'll heat up again.

MORE HOOK-UPS WITH JIGGING SPOONS

Jigging spoons are deadly ice-fishing lures, especially when tipped with a minnow or other live bait. But tipping causes your hooking percentage to drop, because the bait fills up most of the gap of the small treble hook.

The best solution is to replace the treble hook with a single hook. That way, the gap will be much larger. And once a fish is hooked on a single hook, it's much less likely to shake off.

Remove the treble hook from the split ring and replace it with a single hook with a large eye, such as a Kirby. If you use an ordinary single hook, the split ring probably won't fit into the eye.

AFTER THE CATCH

*K*eeping your fish fresh and cleaning them properly will do wonders for the end product.

If your fillets curl up when you put them in the frying pan, you know they're fresh.

KEEPING FISH FRESH

The edibility of your fish depends mainly on what you do with them from the time you catch them to the time you eat them.

Ideally, you would catch the fish, keep them alive until the end of the day, clean them immediately and then toss them into the frying pan.

But for most anglers, that's rarely the way it works.

A more common scenario is to catch some fish early in the morning, put them on a stringer and drag them around for hours after they're dead, clean them late at night or the next day, then stuff the fillets in a plastic bag and freeze them for several months.

After all that, don't expect a lot of rave reviews when your friends stop over for a "fresh" fish dinner.

Here are some tips that will help preserve the table quality of your catch:

SUPER-CHILLING

If you're on a long fishing trip with no access to freezer facilities, keeping the fish you catch the first few days is a problem. They can be kept on ice for maybe 3 days, but not much longer. You can extend the storage time to about a week, however, by super-chilling the fish as shown at right.

Add 1 pound of coarse ice-cream salt to every 20 pounds of crushed ice and place a 4-inch layer of the salt-ice mixture in the bottom of a cooler. Wrap fillets, steaks, or whole gutted fish in aluminum foil or plastic wrap and then place the packages on the salt-ice mixture. Alternate layers of fish and salt-ice and finish with a generous salt-ice layer. The salt-ice mixture has a lower melting point (about 28°F) than regular ice, greatly extending storage time. Be sure to drain the cooler as the ice melts.

CURING HOT-WEATHER WOES

In hot weather, your live well can become a "dead well." When you hook a fish in deep, cool water and then toss it into a live well filled with warm surface water, its life expectancy may be only a few minutes. And you'll have the same problem if you put your fish on a stringer. Here's the best solution:

Rap the fish over the head with a club or "priest" and then put them on a bed of ice in a cooler. The fish will stay fresh until the end of the day. Drain the cooler periodically so the fish do not soak in the meltwater.

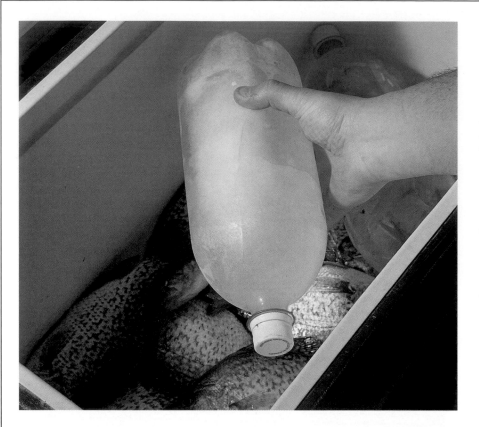

No More Soggy Meat

Your fish can get water-logged if allowed to soak in a cooler full of meltwater from thawing ice. To solve the problem, fill some 2-liter pop bottles with water to within a couple inches of the top and freeze them. Then place 2 or 3 frozen bottles on top of the fish in place of regular ice. The bottles will keep the fish cool without the meat becoming soft and soggy. And as an added bonus, when you get thirsty, you can open a bottle for a swig of ice water.

Handy Freezer Pack

Fish frozen in water keep better than fish frozen dry. Because the meat is not exposed to air, freezer burn is not as much of a problem. Lots of anglers use milk cartons or Tupperware freezer containers for freezing fish in water, but resealable plastic bags work just as well. Just put enough fish for a meal in a bag, fill it with water and then run your fingers across the top while squeezing to seal the bag and expel any excess water. Then label the bag using a waterproof marking pen.

Practical Fishing Tips

SERVING-SIZE FISH BLOCKS

The only problem with freezing fish in water is that you have to thaw out the entire package even if you only want a small portion. Here's the solution:

Place a single layer of fillets or steaks in a resealable plastic bag in a cake pan, add just enough water to cover them, then squeeze out the air and seal the bag. Be sure to leave a little space between the pieces (below left). If desired, stack several bags in the pan before freezing. After the bags are frozen, they can be stacked in the freezer.

Now you can easily crack off single pieces of fish as needed, being careful not to rip the bag (below right). After removing what you need, reseal the bag and put it back into the freezer.

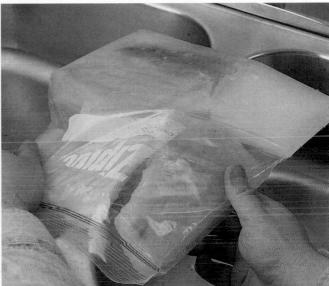

EXTEND FREEZER LIFE

No matter how you freeze your fish, they'll lose their fresh flavor within several months and start to develop a strong, fishy taste as a result of oxidation and bacterial contamination. The oilier the fish, the faster the off taste develops.

You can dramatically slow this deterioration process, however, by soaking the fish in a solution of ascorbic acid, which is available at most drugstores. Just add 2 tablespoons of the acid per quart of water and soak the fish for about 20 seconds before freezing them. If you can't find the acid, you can substitute lemon juice.

FISH-CLEANING TIPS

There are almost as many ways to clean fish as there are kinds of fish. The intent here is not to demonstrate every possible fish-cleaning method, but to show you some tricks that will save you time and make your fish more palatable.

You'll also learn how to get rid of bothersome bones, reduce the level of contaminants and make cleanup easier.

Many anglers don't realize that they're discarding some of the tastiest meat on the fish they clean. We'll give you some little-known tips on how to make the best use of all of your catch.

CANADIAN FILLETING METHOD

Most anglers fillet their fish by removing the sides with rib bones intact and then making another cut to remove the rib bones. But when you're dealing with large fish or fish with heavy rib bones, this method dulls your knife in a hurry.

If you use the Canadian filleting method shown below, however, your knife will stay sharper and you'll get the job done faster because the rib bones are removed with the initial cut. For best results, be sure to use a very sharp fillet knife.

1 Cut behind the pectoral fin and gill cover down to the backbone. Angle the cut toward the top of the head as shown so you don't waste the thick meat behind the head.

2 Make a cut along one side of the back; the tip of your knife blade should just scrape the rib bones but not cut through them.

3 When your knife reaches the end of the rib cage, push it all the way through the fish and then run it along the backbone to free the rear portion of the fillet.

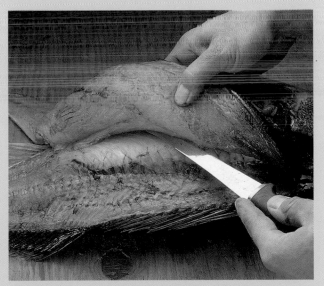

4 Make a series of light cuts around the outside of the rib cage to remove the rest of the fillet. Keep the blade as close to the ribs as possible so you don't waste meat. Repeat the procedure to remove the other fillet.

REMOVING Y-BONES

Lots of anglers turn up their noses at northern pike and pickerel because of those pesky Y-bones. But those bones can easily be removed, leaving delicious white, flaky meat.

There are two different methods for removing the bones, both of which produce excellent results.

If you don't clean pike or pickerel the right way, you'll have to pick out the Y-bones.

Removing Y-Bones: Six-Piece Method

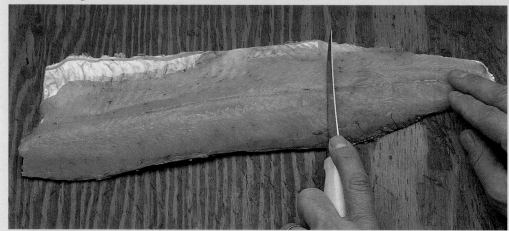

1 *Fillet the fish as you normally would and remove the rib cage. Then run your finger along the inside of the fillet to find the end of the row of Y-bones (blue spots). Cut off the boneless tail section just behind the spot where the Y-bones ended.*

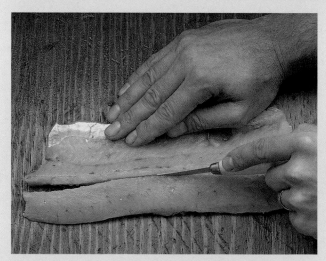

2 *Make a cut along the lower edge of the Y-bones to remove the bottom part of the fillet.*

3 *Make another cut along the top edge of the Y-bones, angling your knife as shown to follow the contour of the bones. Repeat the procedure on the other fillet. You now have 6 boneless pieces of meat. Discard the small strips of meat (bottom pieces) containing the Y-bones.*

Removing Y-Bones: Five-Piece Method

1 With the fish resting on its belly, make a vertical cut just behind the head. Then run your knife along the backbone, stopping just ahead of the dorsal fin. Make another vertical cut just ahead of the dorsal fin to remove the "backstrap."

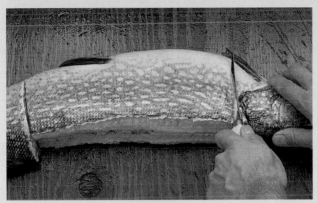

2 Extend the vertical cuts down the side of the fish, cutting down to the backbone.

3 Run your finger along the back to find the ends of the Y-bones (blue spots), then cut along the top of the row of bones to remove the side fillets.

4 Remove the boneless tail fillets.

5 Skin all 5 pieces. Be sure to loosen the skin along the edges of the top fillet so it lies flat before you attempt to skin it.

FIELD DRESSING TROUT

Trout keep a lot better if you field-dress them immediately after they're caught. Here's a slick method that enables you to gut-and-gill a small- to medium-sized trout (or salmon) in just a few seconds:

1 Cut through the thin membrane connecting the throat tissue to the lower jaw.

2 Make a cut along the belly starting at the vent and ending between the pectoral fins. Do not puncture the stomach or intestines.

3 Hold the head with your thumb in the V on the underside of the jaw. Push your other thumb into the body cavity and pull the gills and guts toward the tail to remove them.

4 Scrape out the kidneys (the dark line along the top of the body cavity) using a spoon.

MINIMIZING CONTAMINANTS

It's almost impossible to get away from all contaminants in the fish you catch. Even fish from some remote Canadian waters have surprisingly high contaminant levels. One way to minimize contaminant intake is to eat only smaller fish that have not had time to accumulate so many pollutants. If you want to eat the larger fish, you can reduce your consumption of contaminants by cleaning the fish properly.

Luckily, many types of pollutants, such as PCBs and DDT, concentrate in the oily tissues (dark areas in cross-section below) and can be trimmed away when you clean the fish. However, other substances (like mercury) are equally distributed throughout the fish and cannot be removed.

No More Mudline

Some anglers refuse to eat white bass and other fish that have a dark "mudline" along the side (above), claiming the fish have an oily or muddy taste. But the eating quality of these fish can be greatly improved if you clean them properly:

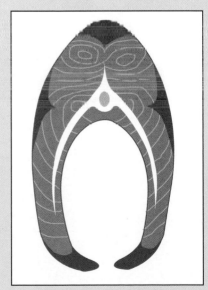

Trim away oily tissues (dark areas) to reduce the potential level of pollutants in any fish you clean.

Using a very sharp knife, remove the fillets and then tilt the blade up slightly when skinning (top). The idea is to leave a thin layer of meat on the skin. This gets rid of most of the dark, oily meat. There may still be a narrow strip of dark meat along the lateral line, but it can be removed with a V-shaped cut (bottom).

No Smell

Don't know what to do with the offal when you're cleaning fish? If the garbage man is coming soon, it's not a problem. But what if he isn't? Here's an easy fix: Clean your fish on newspaper and, when you're finished, wrap the carcasses in the paper, seal it with a piece of tape and freeze it. Take it out right before the next garbage pick-up.

Eliminate E-Bones

When you fillet a fish, you get rid of most (but not all) of the bones. In many gamefish species, a small row of *epiplueral ribs* (E-bones) lies just above the rib cage. Here's how to get rid of them:

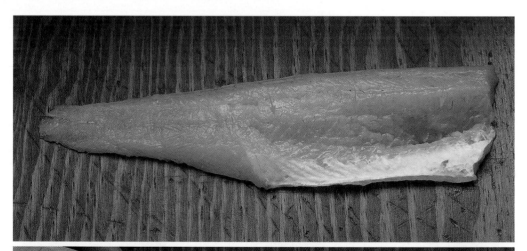

Find the row of E-bones by running your finger along the midline of the inside of the fillet (top photo). Then make a V-shaped cut extending to the rear of the row of bones to remove them (bottom photo).

USING ALL OF YOUR WALLEYE

Walleyes are tops in the frying pan, but most anglers throw out some of the tastiest parts of the fish: the cheeks and the throat latch, or "butterfly." The cheek meat (usually from large walleyes) has been compared to scallops; the butterfly, to shrimp. Here's how to remove these tasty tidbits, which have a chewier texture than the fillets:

How to Remove the Cheeks

1 *Make a cut under the cheek meat, starting at the rear. Stop the cut just behind the eye.*

2 *Pull on the meat to peel it off the skin.*

How to Remove the Butterfly

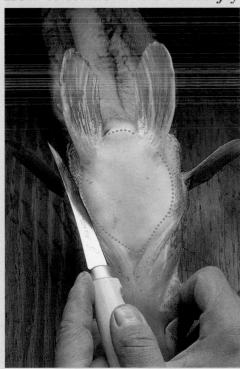

1 *After the fish has been filleted, make a triangular V-shaped cut as indicated by the dotted lines.*

2 *Remove the butterfly with scales and pectoral fins still intact. Fry the butterfly as is; do not attempt to scale or skin it.*

INDEX